THE MOST IMPORTANT HOUR
OF YOUR LIFE

To Jo Thanks for reading.

Paul Sherwood.

The
Most Important
Hour
of
Your LIFE

**FIND YOUR PURPOSE
YOUR POWER AND
THE PATH TO EVERYTHING YOU WANT**

PAUL ISHERWOOD

To us all. That we may take delight in
who we really are and enjoy that path
to everything we really want.

All this and more I wish especially for
my children.

Acknowledgments

To all those who have inspired me along the way. In particular, Tony Robbins, whose audio programs helped me to believe that life could be better and that I was capable of so much more; Neale Donald Walsch whose inspirational books gave me so much insight and a new way of looking at things; and Jerry and Esther Hicks whose life-changing work gave me the insight, clarity and belief that made the writing of this book possible and continues to inspire me to this day. And finally to Ken Heaton, for his immediate proof-reading and prompt supportive feedback.

"If I have seen further it is by standing on the shoulders of giants."

Sir Isaac Newton

Contents

Chapter 8

Chapter 9

Chapter 10

Preface

Wow! It has been a wonderful and amazing journey. My desire to understand life and how to find happiness and success has been pulsing through my veins for as long as I can remember. I dreamed of being rich and always being kind and nice to people; I imagined being happy, enjoying life and being successful.

At the age of 23 I had it all in many ways: I hadn't made my first million but I had graduated from university, had a good job, money, nice house, Golf GTI and my whole life ahead of me. However, I couldn't escape the feeling that there must be more to life than a good job, getting a nicer car and a bigger house. So I quit my job, sold everything, bought a backpack and a ticket to travel the world. Within a few short months, I was on a British Airways flight from London to New York in the hope of finding a job I liked, becoming successful and discovering the secret to a happy life.

25 years later and here I am! Over these years I have come to a powerful understanding of life, its purpose and how you can create the life you want. I have had many experiences, in many countries, as I searched in my quest to find how to live a happy, exciting, rich and successful life. I researched the origins of religion, mysticism, philosophy and psychology. I read many books on spirituality, reincarnation and life after death, as I strived to understand the purpose of life, the nature of the universe and the existence of God.

I studied meta-physics and quantum physics; I read book after book following my desire for understanding and allowed myself to follow my intuition and inspiration wherever it took me. I searched the internet and listened to audiobooks in every available moment; studying books on motivation and success, self-help books and books about becoming rich. I gained so much insight and understanding and yet this led to still more questions as I searched to understand life.

Numerous authors and teachers inspired me during my years of study and research; you can see these sources in the bibliography but this is not meant as a possible reading list. The bibliography represents the twists and turns of my own path of inspiration, as I searched for answers and understanding. In the same way, you are on your own path and as you read this book you will find many of your own inspirations and will be guided on the next steps of your journey: to become who you want to be and to create the life you want to live.

In particular, I was so excited when I discovered *The Science of Getting Rich* by Wallace D. Wattles. The essence of his teaching being that success, and indeed getting rich, was not only possible, it was our birthright; and we get everything we desire by "thinking in a certain way." When Wattles wrote his book, around the turn of the 20th century, there were many other authors of what was called the new thought movement: other notable examples being Napoleon Hill whose best selling book *Think and Grow Rich* was the fruit of his 25 year research into success by interviewing the richest and most successful people of his time; Charles F. Haanel who wrote the *The Master Key System*; and William W. Atkinson, author of *Thought Vibration or the Law of Attraction in the Thought World*. Some time later, as I watched *The Secret* by Rhonda Byrne, I saw that her journey in making *The Secret* began with the discovery of *The Science of Getting Rich* and subsequent study of other new thought authors.

Over these years of research and study I

felt that I had so much wisdom, understanding and insight; and yet there was something missing. I still struggled with my own life, its meaning and how to find success and happiness. I discovered more and more insights that made sense but still not enough to change my life significantly. Then finally, after years of searching and study, I discovered a profoundly clear and powerful understanding: *The Teachings of Abraham* presented by Jerry and Esther Hicks. My years of study allowed me to recognise the power, clarity and importance of these teachings.

As I studied, I received answer after answer to my long held questions. As a result, many things began to fall into place: I gained great confidence, felt more control over my life, felt happier than I had in years and had clarity and vision for my life. I knew I could finally begin to live the dreams I had for my life. At the same time, I recognised the power of these insights to help anyone understand life and how to find happiness and success. At this point, I became clear that a large part of my dream was to write this book and to share and teach this amazing understanding.

As I write this preface I have just been listening to *Walking on Sunshine* and I feel so wonderful, happy and full of life. Yet this is not just because of the music; most days I am feeling the best I have ever felt. I feel confident in my understanding of life and my purpose in life. I wake up looking forward to each day and witness my life getting better and better. I have a vision for my life that fills me with enthusiasm and a knowing that life is working out for me. I spend my days appreciating and enjoying more and more aspects of my life. I feel calmer and stress free most of the time. I feel an increasing sense of freedom, and confidence; I have a greater appreciation of myself and I feel healthier than ever before. I am finding more and more things working out for me; even money coming into my experience in unexpected ways. All this and my book has not even been published yet!

My life is truly magnificent in so many ways and the reason I feel so good about telling you this is because I know that you can come to feel this way about your life.

It is my wish for you to enjoy the journey through these pages as much as I have enjoyed writing them. Look for what feels good to you and you will find answers to your questions and inspirations to make your life better and better.

Paul

Introduction

I am so happy and excited to reveal to you this wonderful and powerful understanding that will allow you to take control of your life. Contained in this book is everything you need to begin to feel good, fill your life with happiness and make your life the way you want it to be. You will come to understand the secret to success; the purpose of your life and how you and you alone, have the power to shape your life and create the life you want.

The most important hour of your life is the time for you to get more of what is most important to you and the time to make your life better in ways that matter most to you. Therefore it is most important that you take the time, first of all, to become clear about what is most important to you and what you really want out of your life. As you read this book you will find yourself becoming clearer about your priorities, about what you really want and you will discover a vision for your life.

What do you want out of your life and what is most important to you? Do you want to feel in control of your life? Do you want to feel good about yourself? Do you want to feel less stressed? Do you want more wonderful things like: beautiful holidays, a lovely car, a beautiful house and delightful friendships? Do you want more love, happiness, fun, joy and laughter?

The most important hour of your life is time to remember your dreams and how you want life to be. You may have been dissuaded from your dreams or you may have concluded that your dreams were unrealistic and should be forgotten. However, your dreams contain your deepest desires and contain the secrets of how you really want your life to be. So the most important hour is a time of discovery, of remembering your dreams and remembering who you really are.

The most important hour of your life is also time to address the most important questions of your life: what brings you most happiness, what is most important to you, what is your purpose, what do you really want and how can you make your life better? Only when you can answer these questions can you begin making your life the way you want it to be and feeling the way you want to feel.

The good news is that you can make your life the way you want it to be and it does not depend on good luck. You will see that contrary to how things look, there is nothing random in the universe or in our lives: everything follows universal law. You will come to understand how the universe was created by the powerful universal law of attraction that also operates in your own life. With this understanding you will see how you can create your reality and make your life the way we want it. As unrealistic as it may sound, the insights presented here will show you that you can be, do or have whatever you want: you can realise your dreams and live an amazing life.

What would be amazing for you? Living on an island in the Bahamas? Cocktails on the beach? Holidaying in beautiful hotel? What would you love to do? Would you love to travel the world? Do you want to be a musician? Do you want wonderful friendships and love? What are your dreams?

You are about to discover that you have the power to create your life the way you want it to be and that is why you have dreams and crave for your life to be better. This book reveals powerful insights into why life is supposed to be good for you, how you can create the life you want and the reasons why your life may not be as good as you want it to be.

You will come to see that the way you think is the key to making your life the way you want it to be and how your thinking and your beliefs have been the deciding factor in making your life the way it is. You will discover how you can gain control of your thoughts and emotions, how life is actually meant to be good for you and that you have the power to attract whatever you desire into your life.

As you read this book for the first time I recommend that you read it in order, as the concepts in each chapter build upon the understandings of the previous chapters. The first chapters explain a powerful understanding of the forces involved in the creation of the universe and how these same forces operate in our own lives. The later chapters explain clearly how this understanding can be applied and used in your own life, how you can begin to make your life the way you want it to be and how you can move in the direction of your dreams.

As important, interesting and powerful as these concepts are, you don't want to just read about your life being better; you want to actually make your life better and live a better life. That is why the most important hour of your life is not just the time to read this book: it is also the time you spend each day doing the things that will improve your life and make it the way you want it. For this reason, you will find many ideas and activities that you can use each day to get more of what is most important to you and to make your life the way you want it to be. We are all different and have unique goals and desires, so chances are that you may not resonate with everything written here, yet if you are open, you will find much of what you have been looking for.

As you apply this understanding to your life, you will witness your life getting better and better in many different ways. We are all at different points in our lives, we have different backgrounds and unique desires, so our lives will get better in different ways. You might begin to feel better about life and about yourself. You might appreciate things more and feel more optimistic. You might see your life being filled with more things that feel good. You might be inspired to change the way you live; you might find a stronger desire to have fun in your life or you might discover a new zest for life.

Throughout my research I was always striving to discover what was most important in life. What you have in your hands is the most powerful understanding that will allow you to get more of what is most important to you. For this reason, the time you spend reading this book and the time you spend each day applying the insights presented here is *The Most Important Hour of Your Life*.

Chapter 1

The Origin of the Universe

There is nothing more important to us than we are happy and that we feel good. We all want the variety of positive good feeling emotions like: happiness, excitement, joy, passion, love, contentment, fulfilment, etc. In fact, everything we do in our lives, we do because we hope that in doing it, or having it, we will feel an improvement in how we feel.

We look around us everyday and we see what we like and what we don't like. We want to feel successful and that our life is good in comparison to what we see around us. In this way, we decide what we want for ourselves. We want more and more of the good things in life; we want our life to make us feel good; we want our life to be as good as it possibly can be.

We all want to have a good life and we all want to be successful but we often doubt whether this is possible. We think a great life might be possible for a fortunate few but probably not for us. Most people don't really believe their life could be how they want it to be.

We have all had dreams and hopes for a great and successful life, but all too often our dreams have faded away. Perhaps we concluded that life could not be that good and through life's challenges and problems we decided to accept that life was just difficult and that our dreams were unrealistic.

All too often, our life becomes a self-fulfilling prophecy and our life becomes as disappointing and difficult as we feared it would be. It seems that as we think about our life, we anticipate how it will be, and unwittingly, create it the way we thought it would be.

To prevent ourselves from creating a life of disappointment, we need a new vision for our life that we can believe in. To create a good life and get more of what we want, we need to believe it is possible. However, just believing it is possible for us to get the life we want is not enough. Most people believe it is possible that they could stumble upon some good fortune and their life could be better but I want to give you something much more powerful.

I want to give you an understanding, belief and conviction that your life is supposed to get better and will get better. I will show you that not only can life be good for you, but life is actually supposed to be good for you.

Before we can believe that life is supposed to be good for us, we need some evidence to back up this new belief and that is what we will be looking at here. Once we believe that our life is supposed to be good for us, we will be in a better position to create the life we want because this is the way we believe it should be.

In order to back up the claim that life is supposed to be good for you, we will start at the beginning. We will look at the way the universe was created, how life came into being and the purpose of life. It is surprising how much science has come to understand about our universe and how life came about. It is even more surprising, how this knowledge helps us to understand the meaning and significance of our own lives, and how life is meant to be: this is a very exciting and enlightening journey. So let's get started and see why life is supposed to be good for you.

Creation of the Universe

According to the latest scientific theory and research, the beginning of our universe was a chaotic one. All the stars, planets and even life itself, began as a chaotic cloud of particles, gas and dust. Some of these particles collided with each other and formed bigger particles. More and more of these particles of matter began to attract and coalesce, eventually forming galaxies, solar systems and our earth.

Newton's law of Gravitation and Einstein's Theory of General Relativity explain that there is a force of attraction between every particle in the universe. The law of gravitation also states that the larger the mass, the greater its force of attraction to itself. Thus science explains that the planets, stars and galaxies were formed because everything was brought together by this universal force of attraction.

This force of attraction is at the heart of the creation of everything in the universe. It is called the universal law of attraction because it acts consistently and universally.

As we shall see, there is evidence of how the universal law of attraction influences and shapes everything; from the formation of planets, to a profound impact on the way we think, how we feel and the life we live.

First we will consider the power and significance of the law of attraction in the creation of the planets and our physical universe. Then we will be in a better position to appreciate how the law of attraction affects us personally.

In the early universe, through the force of

attraction, particles began joining together. As some masses got larger and heavier, they had a stronger force of attraction on the particles of matter that were moving past them. More and more particles were caught in the attractive fields of these growing masses, each mass creating a vortex of attraction, much like a whirlpool, pulling more and more mass, dust and particles towards their centres. Thus larger and larger masses were created, some of which became planets and stars. This familiar spiral shape can be seen to this day, in the familiar shape of our galaxies, as systems of stars and planets travel a spiral path, orbiting the centre of each galaxy.

Our solar system is also a clear illustration of the law of attraction, as the spinning planets remain in orbit, attracted to the sun in the centre, rather than flying off into the distance. This is the universal law of attraction keeping everything in perfect balance. It is therefore not surprising that the formation of our solar system, just like the galaxies, is also a story of the law of attraction.

Before our solar system came into being there was just a chaotic cloud of dust and gas, that scientists call a nebula. Once again the universal law of attraction continued its work and masses were attracted together, until a larger central mass was formed. This central mass attracted more and more to itself. It became bigger and bigger, and exerted a stronger and stronger force, attracting to itself. As this mass got bigger, it attracted particles towards its centre with such force that the centre increased in pressure and temperature. This mass eventually became what we call the sun. Our sun actually contains more than 99% of the mass of our solar system.

As the sun formed, there were still other particles, gas and debris swirling around the sun. This orbiting debris also started to attract to each other and began to form clumps of matter. The bigger the clumps became, the stronger the force of attraction they exerted on the materials around them. Eventually the attraction power of these larger clumps attracted and combined with other clumps, forming larger pieces of rock orbiting around the sun, at various distances from the sun. As the force of attraction pulled the rock together with ever increasing intensity, the larger orbiting rock clumps became more spherical in shape. These spherical clumps of rock became the planets of our solar system.

Evidence of the immense force of attraction can be found in the centre of the earth: the rock has been pulled to the centre of the earth, with such force that the rock remains molten to this day, even billions of years after it was formed.

Universal Intelligence

When you look at the beauty and harmony

of our solar system, and consider that it was formed out of chaotic cloud of dust and gas, it is truly miraculous. The universe, our solar system and the earth are so incredible in their order and perfection. It is amazing to consider that the earth is a ball of rock, spinning on its own axis and travelling around the sun. The perfection of this spinning orbit is such that it has been doing this perfectly for billions of years.

Contemplating the perfection of the solar system and understanding how the earth came into existence is not usually high on our list of priorities however, our daily lives are preoccupied or even consumed with our own feelings, issues and things to do. Yet understanding the nature of the universe is so important in helping us to understand the fundamental nature of life, how life works and how we can create our own life.

The creation of our galaxies and solar system is evidence of the power of the law of attraction. It is important to comprehend this most powerful and universal law because as we shall see, it has the same powerful influence on every aspect of our lives. It is also just as important to consider the origin of this law of attraction. What could be the source of the law that brought this universe together in such an incredible way? Could this amazing universe have been formed through a string of billions of chance, unbelievably lucky coincidences? Could it just be good luck that we see such beauty, harmony and perfection in the universe, solar system and on earth?

Just as many great thinkers have said, there has to be an intelligence beyond our understanding that is behind the incredible complexity, beauty and perfect harmony of the universe. Albert Einstein echoed this sentiment:

> *"Everyone who is seriously involved in the pursuit of science becomes convinced that a spirit is manifest in the laws of the universe, a spirit vastly superior to man..."*

Einstein also wrote of scientists feeling:

> *"... a rapturous amazement at the harmony of natural law, which reveals an intelligence of such superiority that compared with it, all systematic thinking and acting of human beings is an utterly insignificant reflection."*

In other words, there has to be a superior intelligence behind the creation of the universe. This is a most important statement to consider, for if it is true, it is fundamental in understanding the nature of the universe and our lives; and everyone is interested in how to make sense of life and how to make life better. This discussion is not just about being amazed by the universe; it is about understanding the universe, so that we can make our life amazing.

Life on Earth

Let us investigate the proposition that there is a superior intelligence, design and purpose behind the creation of the universe and to life itself. To do this we will look at the formation of the earth and the astonishing circumstances that lead to the creation of the perfect place for life to flourish.

Earth epitomises beauty, harmony and perfection of design. It has beautiful landscapes, flowers, trees, sunrises and sunsets, magnificent oceans, a fascinating array of life forms and it all works together harmoniously and perfectly. Many people have said that this alone is evidence enough of a superior intelligence.

Throughout history, people of science, philosophy and religion have sought to understand the nature and purpose of life, and that is what we are about to consider. We will look at how modern scientific understanding sheds more light on how the earth and life itself came into being. We will then see how it appears that the earth was designed perfectly for life and that there is superior intelligence behind the creation of life on earth.

The rare and magnificent design of the earth is wonderfully described by professor Iain Stewart in the BBC series Earth: The Power of the Planet. The final episode of the series explains how amazing it is that the Earth exists as it does, and the "outrageous good fortune" it has taken.

The program describes how the earth is exactly the right distance from the sun, so that we have the right temperature on earth. Without this relatively mild temperature range, we would not have liquid water; an essential component for life. In fact, the temperature on earth is so perfect that you can find water in all three states: liquid water, ice and water vapour.

This is amazing when you consider that the temperature on the surface of the sun is around 5000°C, and the temperature on Pluto, the planet furthest from the sun, is -230°C. Therefore if the earth was any closer to the sun, like Venus, the surface temperature would be around 400 degrees hotter that the hottest desert on earth. This would be too hot for water to exist as a liquid. If the earth was much further away from the Sun, like Mars for example, it would be so cold as to freeze all the water on the planet. So the earth, out of all of that chaos is in just the right place and just the right temperature for life.

For life as we know it to exist, we need many conditions. For example, we need oxygen, water, and other gases. Well it just so happens that we have the perfect atmosphere around earth containing a perfect mixture of all the gases we need. But there is something you have probably not considered: Why do these gases not just float off our spinning planet and disappear into space? If this happened, there would be no life on earth. However, we still have these gases because the earth is exerting a gravitational force of attraction on the gas molecules. It just so happens that the force of attraction is the perfect strength to keep the gases within a few kilometres of the earth's surface: this is what we call our atmosphere. If the earth was a smaller planet, like Mars, it would exert a smaller force of attraction and the gases we need for life would leak away into space.

Our atmosphere containing oxygen, carbon dioxide and water vapour, etc. creates the perfect living environment on earth. It provides a wonderful climate, the perfect variety of weather, and protection from the harmful rays of the sun. Not only does the atmosphere perform this function perfectly, have you noticed how beautiful the sky is - whether it is pure brilliant blue, a fascinating cloud formation or a majestic sunset? Our weather and climate add a richness to our lives that allows us to live within a beautiful variety of conditions, from playing in the snow, to sunning ourselves on a beautiful beach. All of this has been maintained in perfect harmony for billions of years. Our spinning rock has evolved into the most beautiful awe-inspiring oasis in an otherwise baron expanse of space.

We also have a pretty amazing moon. Would you believe that our moon was also formed into a beautiful sphere through the force of attraction, attracting and fusing smaller particles of rock together that were once orbiting around the earth? That is amazing in itself, but that is just the beginning.

There is also a force of attraction between the earth and the moon that has kept the moon spinning perfectly around the earth. Our moon is also very special because it is the perfect size and distance from the earth. Compared to other moons, our moon is unusually large with respect to its parent planet, earth. It is also unusually close, as compared to other planets and their moons. And guess what? This works out just right! The close proximity and relatively large size of our moon means the force of attraction that the moon exerts on the earth, keeps the earth stable in its orbit around the sun. Without this stabilising influence, the earth would wobble as it orbits around the sun, which would result in dramatic shifts in the earth's climate that would make it very difficult, if not impossible, for life to flourish.

The moon's force of attraction on the earth can be seen by its effect on the oceans. The pull of the moon creates the ebb and flow of our tides and the waves that crash beautifully on our beaches. Notice again how the attractive force that pulls on the oceans is calculated to perfection. It is just right to make the most wonderful waves all around our planet. Can you imagine how bland our oceans would be without waves? On the other hand, what if we had huge tidal waves all the time? Thankfully, the size of the moon and its gravitational pull are perfect: producing a variety of beautiful waves, from waves that wash up gently on our feet, to powerful crashing waves that delight surfers around the world. These waves that land on our beaches are so wonderful and enchanting that we never tire of watching and enjoying their infinite rhythmic beauty.

If you could give the earth a perfect gift, the moon would be it. And doesn't the moon look so beautiful in the night sky whether it is crescent shaped or bright and full?

Now for my final use of the moon as an illustration of the perfect design of the solar system. The orbits of the earth and moon around the sun are such that we enjoy the moon blocking the sun to produce a total solar eclipse. This is where the moon perfectly and completely covers the sun for a short moment in time. This might not sound so special, but it takes perfect mathematical design to make a total solar eclipse possible.

For a total solar eclipse to happen, the sizes

of the sun and moon and their relative distances from the earth have to be just right. And guess what? The mathematics work out perfectly again. The sun is 400 times further away from the earth than the moon and the sun is 400 times bigger than the moon. Therefore from the earth, the sun and moon appear the same size, which is what makes the total solar eclipse possible. For the total eclipse to be possible, not only must the sun and moon appear to be the same size in the sky, their orbits need to be perfectly aligned. And they are! Another coincidence and good fortune?

In terms of perfection of design, it is not just that it is mathematically perfect: it is awe-inspiring and the whole spectacle is described by those who observe it as a most beautiful and magical event. As the first rays of the sun emerge from the darkness, a beautiful "diamond ring" effect is seen. This is only possible, thanks to the perfect size and position of the sun and moon relative to the earth.

In the BBC program, Wonders of the Solar System, Professor Brian Cox expressed much more than his intellectual understanding, as he witnessed a total solar eclipse in India. He was noticeably and understandably awe struck by the event, as were thousands of other observers. He expressed the powerful emotional impact he felt, as he said: "That's the solar system coming down and grabbing you by the throat."

The point of this brief investigation has been to highlight the mathematical perfection and infinite beauty of the universe and to show how this points to there being an intelligence behind the wonder of the world we live in. This is difficult to comprehend from our limited physical perspective, however, the perfection of design, the infinite complexity, and endless nature of the universe, suggests that the intelligence behind it is universal and infinite.

Chapter 2

The Purpose of Life

The purpose of this chapter is to show that the formation of the earth was no accident: the earth in all its magnificence and beauty is the way it is because it has been designed this way. The earth has been designed to be a most beautiful place in which to live because life is supposed to be good.

In fact, throughout history, humankind has always felt that life is supposed to be good. For this reason humanity has created so much wonder and beauty. We have created beautiful homes, clothes, cars, magnificent structures, technology and all the things we want for a better life. We have created holiday experiences, beautiful life styles, music, dance, art and so many other wonderful creations as we follow, unfailingly, our innate desire to make life better.

We never stop wanting more and more wonder and beauty in our lives. This is because we feel profoundly that life is supposed to be good for us. That is why we feel so bad when our life isn't as good as we want it to be.

We want things to be better and better, and this is how it has always been. From the very beginning, there has been evolution and constant improvement. The universe evolved from gaseous chaos to the formation of the stars, galaxies and our solar system. Earth evolved from a spinning ball of rock to the beautiful paradise we live in. Life on earth has evolved from microscopic bacteria to the complex beauty and harmony of the natural world. And the evolution of life continues, as humanity strives every day for a better and better life.

As we go through our days, we constantly see things we want, things we want to improve and we think about how we would like our lives to be. We see constant reminders of ways in which life could be better for us. This is because life is made this way and we cannot stop wanting our life to evolve and get better.

If the world is made in all its magnificence by an infinite intelligence, then like anything created, it must have been created with a purpose. Let us investigate and uncover the answer to our most important question: what is the purpose of life?

There is so much wonder and beauty in our world. Everything works together so harmoniously and brilliantly and there is so much for us to discover, create and enjoy. We know this because we are equipped with all our senses, intellect and consciousness, to appreciate and enjoy all that life on earth has to offer.

There is so much for us to enjoy and there is nothing we want more than to spend our time enjoying it. What we want more than anything else is to feel good or improve how we feel. We might want to do something, buy something or talk to someone, but we always hope to feel better by the experience: none of us set out to feel miserable. All our choices and decisions are made based on what we think will make us feel better. Ultimately, we want to have and experience positive feelings, such as: happiness, freedom, excitement, love, passion, satisfaction, worthiness, power, etc. We want to appreciate and enjoy beauty; we want to have fantastic delicious experiences.

It makes sense that life is supposed to be good for us, because the universe is made in such a way that there are so many things for us to desire, enjoy, appreciate and feel good about. We want to find people we feel good with, we want our body to feel good and we want to eat and drink things that feel good. We have physical senses that are designed to allow us to enjoy the sensations of sight, sound, taste, touch and smell. Through every organ and every sensor in our body, we hope to find something that will feel good.

Life is Supposed to be Good for You

Life is supposed to be good for you because the universe and life are created this way by an infinite intelligence. This infinite intelligence is the reason we have such complex beautiful bodies and brilliant minds. Our bodies and minds crave for life to be good: we have a profound craving for life to be good because we have been designed that way.

Everything points to the fact that life has been designed to be good for us. This is even shown from the time we are born. Babies are born with a knowing that life is supposed to be good for them: they expect everything to be taken care of; they demand that they are comfortable and have a good rest; they demand food when they are hungry; they want love and to be entertained; and they even expect someone to get them cleaned up and dressed! This is what babies expect, and for the most part they get what they want.

We are born into this world knowing that life is supposed to be good for us, and we keep this belief as we grow and progress through our childhood: we just want to play and have fun. We have no inclination to strive to be responsible or to work hard; we just want to do what feels good.

Children want to feel loved and secure and then go out and play. Children still know that life is supposed to be good for them and nothing is more important than they feel good. This is why children get over arguments quickly, because they know it is the quickest way to get back to playing, having fun and feeling good again. Children know at the very core of their being that life is about feeling good.

Life is supposed to be good for you and life is supposed to feel good. You want this more than anything. You want your life to be good and you always want it to improve, evolve and get better.

The Purpose of Life

How does this help us find our purpose of life? The purpose of our life, our reason for existing, must be something we feel profoundly and fundamentally. Our purpose must be that which we consider most important to us: and nothing is more important to us than we feel good. It follows that the purpose of our life is to feel good: to experience all the wonderful things and feelings life has to offer; feelings such as joy, fun, love, wonder, excitement, happiness, exhilaration, passion, etc. And when we feel good, we are in tune with all of life and living our purpose. Yet this is not the end because our desire for joy and feeling good knows no limits. Once we feel good our purpose and desire will be to feel even more joy or a higher level of joy or a different type of joy. Our purpose of life is to experience expanding and evolving joy and good feelings.

Our purpose is to create, live and enjoy a life that feels good and a life that gets better and better. Would you like a life that felt really good? Would you like it to feel good in many different ways? Would you like your life to just remain good or would you like a life that kept delivering new ways to feel good; new delicious experiences and delightful surprises?

Is this too simplistic to be the purpose of life? Or is feeling good just so fundamental, so basic and so important to us, that it must be connected to our purpose for living? After all, when people feel really good, we say they are full of life. On the contrary, it is only when people feel really bad that they no longer want to live.

Consider the reason for creating anything. In creating or making anything we hope to enjoy the finished product and enjoy using it, whether it is a painting, a house or an innovation in technology. We always create something in the hope that it will improve things and that we will enjoy the finished result. We even want to enjoy the process of creating. In the same way, the infinite intelligence behind the creation of life and the universe, did so with a purpose of joy. If an infinite intelligence created with a motivation to feel good, then this explains why the universe is so infinitely beautiful, amazing and awe-inspiring. And that is why, more than anything, humanity strives for happiness, enjoyment and to feel good.

However, if life is supposed to be so good for us, then the big question is - why isn't it?

Why Life Doesn't Feel Good

As we grew up, we received a very different message from our parents, friends and other people around us. It most probably wasn't that life was supposed to be good for us. In fact, we probably heard that life was hard, difficult and in many ways dangerous. We were often told about all the things that we should be careful of and all the things we shouldn't do. We were surrounded by conversations about accidents, illness, crime and anything bad that had happened to someone. The well-meaning adults around us told us everything bad that had happened and that could possibly happen to us, in the hope that this knowledge would help us avoid anything bad happening to us. The bleakest, most dangerous picture of life was painted in order to equip us on our journey through life in a dangerous and uncertain world.

Yet we can hardly blame them: they grew up receiving a similar message of hardship and danger. Since then, they have had the same message emphasised everyday by the news. What else could they do? They cared for us so deeply and wanted us to be safe, healthy and happy.

Those around us may have been frustrated with life and sometimes frustrated with us. As children all we wanted was to focus on fun and what felt good for us; even though at times this got us into trouble. We may have been called silly, naughty or selfish. As we got older we may have received an increasing number of negative messages and criticisms of our behaviour. In a world that values hard work and responsibility above creativity and feeling good, we may have been described as lazy, irresponsible or worse. As we felt the disapproval of others, more than likely, our sense of self-worth and confidence slowly eroded.

Surrounded by a society and world that was focused on what was wrong, bad and dangerous, we slowly lost touch with our natural enthusiasm for life and lost touch with our dreams. We began to get less fun out of life, we found more to complain about and much of the time, life didn't feel so good.

After a lifetime of negative thoughts, worries, fears and concerns, our natural zest and enthusiasm for life has been worn down and our youthful dreams of a wonderful, exciting and successful life have probably faded away.

It is also very common to think and believe that life is random, and that all you can do is work hard and make your life as good as you can. Most of us feel life is very uncertain, where some people are lucky and have a good life, whereas other people are unlucky. Some people even seem to get the exact opposite of what they want in life. On the other hand, there seem to be the fortunate few, who get what they want; they seem to have great lives and are followed by success wherever they go. Some people are living their dreams and get whatever they think about.

Time to Make Your Life Better

In the next chapter, we will look at the power our beliefs exert on what we think and how we create our own lives by the way we think and feel. You will be introduced to incredible insights and understandings that explain that life doesn't need to be so random and uncertain. In fact, our lives are under the influence of the same laws and processes that produced the magnificent world in which we live. Just as the universe was created perfectly, by an infinite intelligence and the universal law of attraction, so are our lives.

If this seems unrealistic, and too good to be true, take a moment to remember that we are on a ball of spinning rock, moving through space, around a huge ball of fire, the heat from which is keeping us alive. Now that's unrealistic - its more like a fairytale! How are we even alive? Think of all that it has taken to create life from a barren ball of rock. Think of all that we need to survive: food, water, oxygen, heat, light, climate, to name but a few. It is a miracle that we have what we need to survive.

Yet life on Earth is far more than just survival. Our life is far more than a 'cosmic fluke,' of life beginning, surviving and maintaining an existence on a ball of rock. Life is absolutely magnificent. It is incredible when you look at the diversity of life, the complexity, and at the same time the beauty, abundance and harmony of life on earth. Then as if that is not enough, think of the complexity and profound nature of human life: our emotions, relationships and our ability to create, evolve and perfectly adapt to life on earth. We have intelligence, consciousness, hopes, desires and dreams.

This is your most important time; your time to see that you have the power to shape your life the way you want it. It is time for you to remember your dreams and remember that life is supposed to be good for you.

Chapter 3

The Power of Your Thoughts and Beliefs

The way we think and what we believe determines our life experience. Indeed our whole life is governed and created by the way we think and the way we feel.

"I think therefore I am."

Descartes

In the last chapter it was stated that life is supposed to be good for you. Think how this way of thinking or this belief might change the way you look at life. If you believed that life was supposed to be good for you, you would expect life to be good and you would look for reasons to make it good.

If we think and believe that life can and

should be good, and indeed that life was designed that way, then it makes sense for us to feel that we are worthy and deserving of a good life. However, there are many times when we do not feel worthy and deserving.

Thanks to our background, we may believe that we do not deserve the wonderful life that we secretly desire. We may have been told many times growing up that we were naughty, badly behaved, greedy, selfish, stupid etc. We may have been influenced by the prevailing beliefs of the society that we grew up in. We may have been told that wanting money and a good life was selfish. We may have been given the message that it was better to think of others than ourselves. On the other hand, we may have learned that we had to be super-competitive, to get ahead in this dog-eat-dog world. We may have picked up many beliefs that emphasise the possible dangers in life and things to be afraid of.

For whatever reason, we may now feel that life is difficult, hard work and probably not going to be that good for us. We may even feel that we are not deserving, and probably not lucky enough to have the life that we truly want.

As we live our life with these beliefs and patterns of thought, we tend to notice many things that prove life to be the way we thought it would be. If we think that life is only good for some people, then these very thoughts are blocking us from everything we want. We can only begin to get the things we want and make our lives better, when we believe we can.

> *"Whether you think you can, or you think you can't - you're right."*
>
> Henry Ford

For us to make our lives better and have the life we want, we first need to be able to feel worthy of a good life and believe that is possible. If we are able to think and feel that we deserve a good life and that life is supposed to be good for us, then we are much more likely to attract the life we want.

So how do we get ourselves to believe this? Well a belief is nothing more than a thought we keep thinking. A belief is a thought or thoughts that we believe are true. We can have a belief about anything, as long as we have enough evidence that we feel justifies and supports it.

As we saw in the first chapters, there is so much evidence to support the belief that life is supposed to be good for us, however, it is more likely for us to give our attention to the reasons why life is not so good. We have become very good at noticing, criticising and complaining about all the things, situations and people we don't like. We have proved to ourselves many times over, that life is not so good. As a result of this thinking, we often feel powerless to change our life and get what we want.

To make changes in our life and to get what we want, we need to change this way of thinking. This is because as we think in a certain way, we are creating our perception of reality, as well as attracting it into our experience. What we think about and how we think creates our experience of life. We create our own reality by the way we think.

> *"We are what we think. All that we are arises with our thoughts. With our thoughts we make the world."*
>
> Buddha

On a common sense level, the way we think about things, and the way we perceive things, creates our experience and how we feel. For example, some people, usually children, perceive snow as wonderful, exciting and the chance of a fun time. Other people may see snow as horrible, cold, miserable and the cause of dangerous roads. So exactly the same situation is thought about in very different ways, by different people: we perceive everything in our own unique way.

The way we think about things and how we perceive life, determines the choices and decisions we make, what we say, what we do and this shapes our whole experience of life. I am not saying that one way of thinking about snow or anything else is right or wrong. What I am saying is that what we think and believe shapes our experience of life. Therefore, it is important that we have thoughts and beliefs that help us in creating the life experience that we want. In fact, we can learn to choose our thoughts and beliefs, and begin to get more control over our life. As we do this more and more, we can begin to create the life we want.

You Feel the Way You Think

So we create our life by the way we think and as we think about things, this determines how we feel. In other words, our thoughts create our feelings. For example, we can't feel angry without first thinking about a situation or person that triggers angry thoughts. As we think more angry thoughts, we start to feel angry. More thoughts are then usually stimulated and we feel even more angry feelings. We can find ourselves feeling worse and worse, the more we think in this way. Often our thinking process is so quick that we don't even realise that we are doing it. We just think we are feeling but there are always thoughts at the root of all our feelings.

For you to feel the feelings of love you have to first think about a person or situation, that stimulates feelings of love. For you to have the positive good feeling of love you must have been thinking positive, appreciative and good feeling thoughts. The more you think loving, wonderful thoughts, the better you feel.

When we feel a certain way, we rarely notice the thinking that started it all. We are too busy experiencing the resulting emotions and the new thoughts that have already flooded our mind. Yet our thinking is always at the root of how we are feeling. Our mood and how we feel are indicators of how we have been thinking.

Let's say for example that you are making plans for a barbecue or garden party and you are going to invite all your friends. You think about all that would make it a great time. You might think about the fun and laughs you would have and perhaps think about the last time you all got together. These thoughts would make you feel good and would inspire a desire within you to have another great time. As you think in this way, you would have so many good feelings, even though the party hadn't happened yet.

Now imagine that you have made the plans and invited your friends for this great time. Then you hear that it is going to rain. As you think about your ruined plans, you begin to feel bad. In an instant, your imagination gives you lots of images of your ruined party. These images are thoughts. You think of people wet and cold, your guests leaving early, wet food etc. Other thoughts fill your mind and before you know it, you feel terrible.

Our thoughts determine how we feel, so at any moment, it is the way we are thinking about the events in our life that dictates how we feel; it is not the events themselves. The way we think and what we think about affects the way we feel, and the way we feel is our experience of life.

In the same way, our beliefs greatly affect our life because beliefs are also a way of thinking: our beliefs are well-practised patterns of thought that also stimulate the emotions and feelings that we have everyday. How we think and feel then dictates what we want and what we do. This is what makes up our life experience - what we think, how we feel, what we want and what we do. In this way, we create our own reality everyday and in every moment.

Have you noticed that the way you feel controls your actions? If you feel really happy, you might feel like going out with friends and having a good time. If you feel down, you may just feel like being on your own. If you feel really nervous about a new situation for example, your nervous feeling may affect your performance and even prevent you from being your normal self.

The good news is that you can improve your life simply by changing how you think. It is possible to think in a way that can begin to improve your life immediately. To do this you need to become more aware of how you think and feel, and to understand that you often have a choice about how you think.

You may doubt that you can have control over your own thoughts because you have had many times when you have felt thoughts flooding into your mind, and you could not stop thinking about something. The reason you feel like this is because your thinking has momentum. As you think a thought, similar thoughts are attracted into your mind; the more you think about something, the more you feel a certain way, the more similar thoughts enter your mind. Such momentum of thoughts means that you cannot suddenly stop thinking about something you feel strongly about. Has anyone ever told you to think positive when you were already feeling bad about something? It doesn't work does it? It's the last thing you want to hear. Your thoughts have a momentum and you cannot suddenly think in the opposite way.

It is also important to be aware that what you focus on or give our attention to, will be triggering your thoughts: what you give your attention to is what you think about; then what you think about determines how you feel; and nothing is more important to you than how you feel.

Chapter 4

The Law of Attraction

Just as the universe was created by the law of attraction, so our lives are created by the law of attraction. This is the fundamental law through which we create our own reality. It is a universal law because is acts on everything, including our thoughts and is evident everywhere.

The law of attraction says, "like attracts like". This is why, when you think in a certain way, you get more of those types of thoughts. So if you start to think about what is wrong with your life, you quickly find other thoughts that show you what you don't like about your life. You develop a train of thought, where one thought attracts another thought. In the same way, as you start to find things you like about your life and you think about these positive aspects, you attract more positive thoughts about your life.

Thoughts really do attract each other and it happens continuously. For example, when you have a conversation with someone, have you noticed how spontaneously the topic of conversation triggers your thoughts? If someone mentions an injury or illness they have just got over, then you remember when something similar happened to you or someone you know and you tell your story. As you talk, the subject of the conversation attracts similar thoughts in you, and then this stimulates and attracts related thoughts in the other person. We usually give very little attention to how we are thinking or where our thoughts are coming from; we just tend to allow our thoughts to take us where they want to go. However, once you see the power of your thinking to create your life, you will want to take more control of your thinking, what you give your attention to, and what you talk about.

You Create Your Own Reality

In contrast to thinking about all the good in our life, we tend to give so much of our attention to the aspects of our life that are not going well. We spend a lot of time worrying and anticipating problems, as well as criticising ourselves and others.

Giving so much of our attention to things that we don't want, has the effect of attracting more thoughts and feelings of the things we don't want. By the universal law of attraction, we are constantly attracting more into our life by what we think about and how we feel. In this way, we create our own reality everyday, and throughout our day.

The question is, are we are creating the life we want, or are we attracting more of what we don't want? The choice is ours. We can allow our mind to constantly criticise and complain, or we can develop a way of thinking that focuses on the positive, on what is going well and what we can appreciate. If we decide to be more positive and appreciative, it will become easier to see all the good in our life and we can begin to believe that life is supposed to be good for us and indeed that life is already good in many ways.

The more good we see in our life, the more good things we attract. If we give our attention and thought to what is going well in our life, what we like about ourselves and anything that feels good, we will attract more of what we want and make our life better and better.

There are many success stories of people believing in their own success, even though all the odds were stacked against them. Are these people just lucky? Why do some people seem lucky, whereas some people seem so unlucky, accident prone, or always seem to miss out? Someone could be unlucky once or twice but why would someone consider himself or herself an unlucky person?

A person is unlucky because they think they are. If something doesn't turn out the way someone hoped it would when it seemed likely to do so, they might consider it unlucky. Yet this is just a way of thinking. If this way of thinking is repeated when other things don't go their way, then this repeated thinking can become a belief. They can believe that they are unlucky. If they believe this, they will even expect to be unlucky. It won't be long before they have another experience where they feel unlucky.

There are also people who seem to be repeatedly lucky. These people are not as common as the 'unlucky' ones. The 'lucky' ones among us, also start with a thought. They might think that things usually go their way, or that they have luck on their side. These people get into the habit of expecting, and even believing that things will go their way. They believe they can get what they want. These successful people seem to give off a vibe of positive expectation, of things going well for them, and the universe seems to respond to their vibe, bringing them what they believe they deserve. This is the universal law of attraction at work. As we think, feel and believe, so it is attracted into our experience. This is how we create our own reality.

Think Your Life Better

If thought attracts similar thoughts then imagine if you were to think that life was supposed to be good for you, and that your life was supposed to get better and better. If you thought this way and believed it, you would expect and anticipate good things to be coming into your life. As you continued to think this way, you would find and attract more thoughts that show you where life is good. At the same time, you would begin to open your eyes to more aspects of your life that were already working out well. You would also start to find more and more that you could appreciate in your life. Your thinking and what you notice would then start to reinforce the thought that life is good.

There are many things and situations that you have in your life now, that in the past were just desires and things you hoped for. We tend to forget these things and give all our attention to the new things we want. It is healthy and natural to have desire and think about the new things we want; it is also important to maintain healthy appreciation for what we already have. In fact, as you are about to discover, feeling good and appreciating what you have now is the path to attracting all the new wonderful things you want in your life.

Through the law of attraction, which says that like attracts like, your thoughts are very powerful because you start to attract similar thoughts. The more you think about something, the more your thoughts build momentum. The way you are thinking, and the way you feel, is how you create your mood. Your mood is like an atmosphere around you or vibe you are giving off. You are giving off a vibrational signal about how you are feeling to the universe and all those around you. In fact, we are not the only ones giving off a vibrational signal - the whole universe is vibrational.

Everything is Vibration

The universe is made up of vibrating energy: every single atom of matter, whether solid, liquid or gas, is actually vibrating. Quantum physics has explained that just like light, sub-atomic particles can behave as waves as well as particles. Furthermore, according to string theory, everything in the universe is made up of tiny vibrating strings. I mention this simply to further emphasise the vibrational nature of our reality.

We are surrounded by vibration everyday of our lives. Whatever we see, is because our eyes are interpreting waves of light, which are a form of vibration. All waves are vibration: when we hear a sound or listen to music, vibrational sound waves make our ear drums vibrate. The ear transforms these vibrations into electrical signals, which are sent to the brain. These electrical signals are also vibration. Even when we think, our brain waves are vibration.

Everything is vibration, including our thoughts. This is not a new concept, for in 1908, William Walker Atkinson wrote: "thought is a manifestation of energy." In his book, *Thought Vibration or the Law of Attraction in the Thought World*, he also explained how the universal law of attraction applies to our thoughts: as we think we attract similar thoughts. In this way we can attract the things we desire, or the things we fear.

The universal law of attraction applies to vibration and everything is vibration. This means that similar vibrations will attract each other. An example of this is when two sounds of a similar frequency attract each other and make a bigger, more powerful sound: this is called resonance. Similarly, when you have something in common with someone, there is an attraction, and we say that we are in tune or on the same wavelength. When we use the words in tune or having the same wavelength, we are saying we have a similar vibration. When we get together with someone on a similar frequency, we feel more energy due to the synergy or resonance of our vibrations.

Now we are at the point where we can look at the universe as being made up of vibration, governed by the law of attraction, where everything is attracting everything else to varying degrees (Newton's law of gravitation and Einstein's Theory of General Relativity mentioned in chapter 1). The force of attraction between some things is indistinguishable, whereas there is a very strong force of attraction between things of a similar vibration. This force of attraction operates in our own life where the way we think and feel attracts more thoughts, situations and people that feel the same.

Without understanding this, we have been quite careless in the way we have been thinking because we have not known that it matters what we think about. We have not known that what we think about we get more of and what we give our attention to and think about, determines how we feel. And we have not known that we live in a vibrational universe, governed by the law of attraction.

The way we think and feel, gives off a vibrational signal that attracts similar thoughts and feelings into our experience. The law of attraction is universal, unfailing and consistent: just like gravity, it is at work whether we are thinking about what we want or what we don't want. Whatever we are giving our attention to is what we are attracting more of into our lives. Therefore it is most important that we choose to think in a way that benefits us and attracts more of what we want into our lives.

It follows that since our beliefs are thoughts that we habitually think, they are also attracting into our experience. If we believe that this world is a dangerous place, and so we give our attention and thinking to all possible dangers, then we attract similar thoughts of danger and we begin to feel worse. We will feel fear more of the time and see more and more possible dangers. If we maintain this thinking and vibration we are much more likely to find ourselves in a dangerous situation or place of fear.

These thoughts of danger and fear are in opposition to the purpose of life discussed earlier: the universe has been designed in all its beauty, harmony and abundance because life is supposed to be good for us. The more we believe and think in this way, the less time and space we have in our mind for our old thoughts and beliefs of insecurity, shortage and fear. With this new understanding, it is time to think and believe in a way that attracts more of what we want and not more of what we don't want.

Chapter 5

You Can Decide to Feel Good

The most important thing for us and that which most affects our life is how we feel. Therefore, it is most important that you start to get control of how you feel. To do this, you need to control what you give your attention to or what you focus on: it is what you give your attention to that determines what you think about and therefore how you feel. In order to gain more control of your thoughts you need to be clear about what you are going to be giving your attention to before you rush into your day. There will be many people and situations that will demand your attention but you always have a choice what you think about or how you think about something. If you want to take control of your life and you want to feel good, then the most important thing for you to do is to decide to give your attention to things that make you feel good. As you think about more things that make you feel good, you will enjoy more good feelings and you will begin to feel better, more of the time. As you feel better more of the time, you will become clearer about what makes you feel good and what you really want out of life. You will feel deeply that what you want more than anything is to feel good and feel good about life.

Once you start on this path of making it a priority that you feel good, you will begin to feel better more of the time and as you feel better, you will attract more thoughts, feelings and situations that make you feel good. These new habits of thought will improve your life day by day and in so many ways.

The best time to start a new habit of thought is in the morning, before you allow yourself to slip into thoughts that don't feel so good; such as how you hate mornings, how you are too tired or how you hate Mondays. This is the time to get out of bed on the right side, by thinking about some things that make you feel good. Choose to give your attention to what you know will make you feel good, as much as possible. Give your thoughts to anything that you can appreciate, be grateful for or feel good about. You will feel much better if you direct your thoughts to appreciating the warmth and comfort of your bed or feeling grateful for the sleep you have had rather than complaining in your mind about having to get up or how cold it is outside.

As you start your day in this way, you are more likely to feel good in your day. You will be more aware of what is going your way, and all that you can appreciate in your day. As you do this, and even make it a habit, you will find it easier to entertain the thought that life is supposed to be good for you.

Throughout your day, you are also creating the life you want by deciding how you want to feel, and the type of things you want to think about. You can only have control over the creation of your life by being aware of your thinking and consciously choosing thoughts that make you feel good.

As you begin your day and go through your day, choose to find things to appreciate and what you can be grateful for. Choose to notice what is going well and anything in your life that you are happy about. There are always things you like and there are always things or people you don't like. There is always a choice between focusing on something you can appreciate or an aspect you can criticise. The point is to give more and more of your attention to things you do like. As you do this, you will notice more and more things you do like, and you will also attract more of what feels good into your life.

So we are in a vibrational universe, created by an infinite intelligence for the purpose of joy and goodness. Our life is supposed to be good and we have been given the power of our own thinking and the freewill to choose our thoughts. We have the control of our own thinking - nobody else. We have control of our own thinking, so we have control how we feel and of our mood. And thanks to the way the universe works, through the universal law of attraction, we have the ability to create our life by the way we think, feel and believe: as we think and feel, we attract.

If we think about what we want, we begin to attract it into our experience. If we think about what we don't want, then this vibration begins attracting more of what we don't want. This does not mean an instant manifestation of something you don't want, but the more you think about something, the more powerful the attraction into your life. Similar thoughts and feelings will be attracted first but ultimately, you will attract physical things, people and situations that match what you have been thinking about

Our thoughts are vibrational, and how we think determines our personal vibration. This vibration is like an atmosphere or vibrational signal we send out. The vibration that we give off is what attracts everything into our experience. Everything that comes into our experience, from thoughts to things, does so in accordance with the law of attraction.

If you want to know how you are vibrating, just look to how you are feeling. If you are feeling good, then your vibration is of a higher frequency and you are attracting more of what will make you feel good. If you are feeling bad, it is an indicator that you have been thinking about things that don't make you feel good and you have a vibration that will be attracting more bad feeling thoughts and things that will not make you feel so good.

The way you are vibrating can also be perceived by those around you. We have all had the experience of observing people and being able to tell if they are in a good mood or not. If you walk into a room where the tensions are high, you can feel it in the air. We truly live in a vibrational universe and we are giving off a vibration and interpreting vibrations all the time.

So your mood, how you feel, your thoughts and your beliefs, determine your life experience. In fact, your mood and how you feel is your life, because if you are in a good mood and feeling great, that's it! That is what you want more than anything.

There is nothing we want more than to feel good. It is the reason we do everything and want everything: we hope to feel better in having the new thing or new situation. What is more, we never stop wanting to feel better. If you are feeling good, then you want to keep feeling good, until fairly soon, you will discover a desire for something new that you think will make you feel even better, or make you feel good in a different way.

Your mood and how you feel is everything. From your good-feeling mood, you get inspiration to do other things that feel good. From your good mood, you will appreciate things more and enjoy things more. You are more fun to be with and people enjoy being with you. You can even deal with setbacks better and when things don't go your way you can keep a calmer perspective. You will also find it easier to believe that things are going to work out for you and that life is good for you; and with this attitude there is a high probability that they will.

It is great to be in a good mood but often we don't keep it going. This is because for whatever reason, something happens or we talk with someone that stimulates thoughts in us that don't feel good. Usually, without realising it, we begin thinking about things in a way that doesn't make us feel good. As we think in this way, we get more thoughts that don't make us feel good and we feel worse: the law of attraction never stops!

It is therefore natural to sometimes find ourselves in a lower mood and not feeling so good. In a low mood, we tend to over-think and analyse our problems and this just makes us feel worse. If we accept that we sometimes don't feel good and it's ok, if we relax and take our mind off the problems, our mood will lift more quickly than if we try to analyse why we are feeling bad. It is better that we don't try to think ourselves out of a low mood. This is described clearly in Richard Carlson's book, *Stop Thinking and Start Living*.

The best time to think in a more positive way is in the morning after we have slept, although even after a nap or some other distraction we stand more chance of thinking in a more positive way and feeling better. As we become more aware of our thinking and how it creates our moods, lower moods will become less common and less prolonged.

Each day we have another opportunity to decide to feel good, and the best time to do this is first thing in the morning. No matter what has gone on the day before, we can again choose thoughts that feel good. We now know that life is supposed to be good for us and that we create our life by the way we think and feel. We have the knowledge to create our life in the way we want it, and we can begin anew each day.

Life and the universe have been created by an infinite intelligence, for the purpose of joy and happiness. If this is true and life is supposed to be good for us, then the universe and infinite intelligence is on our side. The infinite intelligence of the universe wants our life to be good. There is no malevolent force trying to trip us up and make our life miserable. We create our life through our own thinking, and it is only our own thoughts about something that make us feel miserable.

The abundance, beauty and harmony of the universe is a profound message that says: 'your life is supposed to be one of abundance, well-being and beauty.' Remember, the purpose of life is joy and happiness, and life is supposed to be good for you. It follows that the infinite intelligence of the universe, the power that creates worlds, is behind you in your desire to make your life better and better. As if that were not empowering enough, remember that you create your own reality by the thoughts you think, and the universal law of attraction brings everything into your experience in response the vibration of your thinking.

We actually have so much going in our favour. Once we understand that we live in a vibrational universe, governed by the law of attraction and we have the universe on our side, there is no longer any need to see the world as competitive, uncertain and dangerous.

Life is not supposed to be random, difficult and confusing. Yes, there are ups and downs, but every cloud does indeed have a silver lining. Things are always working out for us. Life is supposed to be good for us and life is supposed to get better and better. However we often don't help ourselves and we are often our own worst enemy. In fact, as we create our own reality by the thoughts we think, we are our only enemy, because it is only by our thoughts, feelings, and law of attraction, that we create our whole experience.

Everything that comes to us in our life is because we live in a vibrational universe, responding to the vibration of our thoughts and feelings, by the law of attraction. When we care about how we feel and what we think about, we begin to take control of our life. We begin to make life the way we want it.

Life is supposed to be good for you and life can be really good for you. In fact, you can have, be and do anything you want. After all, if the universe, in its infinite wisdom has inspired desires within you, then infinite intelligence must have the means to deliver your desires to you.

The power to create your life is in your hands. But where do you start? How can you begin to apply this powerful understanding? The next chapters offer practical insight on how to begin creating the life you want. Just concentrate on what feels right to you and what makes sense to you. If some things don't feel right for you then don't give them much attention for now, just focus on the aspects of this understanding that really make sense to you.

Life is supposed to be good for you and you do create your own reality. Any time you spend consciously creating your life the way you want it is surely the most important thing you can do. What could be better or more important than creating a wonderful life for yourself and feeling amazing? The time you spend in the study, understanding and application of the knowledge contained here could therefore be the most important hour of your life.

Chapter 6

You Can Think Your Life Better

Life is supposed to be good for you, and nothing matters more to you than you feel good. You also have the power and ability to create your life by the thoughts you think and how you feel. Of course, what you think and how you feel determines what you say and do, but this is not all: your thoughts are creating a vibrational signal that emanates from you and into this vibrational universe which is continually responding to your vibrational signal in accordance with the law of attraction. Whether you are thinking about what you like or thinking about what you don't like, you are attracting more of what you are thinking about: your life is a reflection of what you have been thinking about.

Your mood or how you feel is also a reflection of how you have been thinking. If you are in a good mood, the atmosphere or signal you are radiating attracts more thoughts and things to help your good mood. If you are in a bad mood, with a dark cloud over your head, you will attract more thoughts and things to keep your bad mood festering. In this way, you attract and therefore create your reality, your experience of life, every moment, of every day.

Begin Creating Your Amazing Life

In this chapter, we will see that not only is life supposed to be good for you but you can in fact create an amazing life; by the way you think, the way you perceive your life, what you believe and what you give your attention to. Just as the universe was created step by step, through the law of attraction, so you can begin creating your ideal life, thought by thought.

The first step in creating your amazing life, is to feel good about your life as it is right now. Begin to make your life the way you want it, by noticing all the things that you can already feel happy about. Practice the art of appreciation, by giving your attention and thinking about things you like and what is good in your life. At the same time avoid finding things to criticise, complain or worry about. If you accomplish this one change, it will have a dramatic effect on your life. And you have not had to do anything, other than change your thinking. Yet this is no small thing, in fact it is a major change, because there is nothing more important than you feel good, and your own thoughts are the key to feeling good.

Now bear in mind that so far in your life, you have been better at noticing and thinking about what is wrong with your life and what you don't like. You have probably, like most people, spent a lot of time thinking or worrying about what is not working out or what might go wrong. Of course, it is ok and normal to notice and acknowledge what you don't like but you will come to see that it is better not to dwell on these things.

It is far better to give more attention to what you do like than what you don't like. In any situation, try to make the best of where you are by looking for the benefits of where you are, rather than what is wrong. As you practise this positive outlook, you will become better and better at finding things to appreciate in any situation. As you do this, you will attract more positive thoughts by the law of attraction. For example, you will get thoughts of expecting good things to come your way and things working out for you.

It is good to become aware of times in your day when you feel good or when you feel in a good mood. Appreciate whenever you are feeling good about something and enjoy the moment. As you give more attention to when you are feeling good, by law of attraction, you will attract more good feeling thoughts and situations that you can feel good about. You will get better and better at this, and you will notice more and more things that you can feel good about. Then as you do this, more good things will come your way as your experience matches the way you have been thinking.

Life is supposed to be good for you and this means that life is supposed to work out for you. Remember, the whole universe and your life have a purpose of goodness and everything is still evolving and getting better. As you begin to appreciate life more, notice more beauty, and feel better, you will be getting in tune with the positive energy of well-being that permeates the world in which you live. As you notice more beauty in your life, you will attract more and notice more. The more you give your attention to the abundance of beauty, harmony and goodness in the world, the more you attract beauty, harmony and goodness into your life. The more you are in tune with the well-being that is available all around you, the better you will feel. As you do this, you will start to experience more moments when you feel good and even wonderful. These delicious, good-feeling thoughts and experiences are the beginning of your amazing life.

Know the Power of Your Thinking

The best time to start making your life amazing, apart from now, is every morning. You see, when you wake, you start your thinking all over again, and this is the best opportunity to find some thoughts that feel good. Often, however, we tend to pickup our thinking right where we left it the previous day. It is very easy for us to remember our worries, fears or concerns that we have been thinking about in previous days. Also, as we wake in the morning, it is easy to pick thoughts that we habitually think; thoughts like, I'm so tired, it's so cold, I hate work, why did I go to bed so late? etc.

Up until now, we have just thought whatever came into our mind without any consideration or understanding of the consequences of our own thinking. This is because we have not known that our thoughts create how we feel; that our thinking creates our personal vibration; that by the law of attraction, our vibration attracts more thoughts, feelings and even situations that match the way we have been thinking; and that in this way, we have been creating our days and our life.

Have you ever noticed when you feel frustrated about something, pretty soon you find something else that is frustrating? Before you know it, you might find yourself feeling angry about something, then something else happens to make you feel worse; perhaps you bang your toe or break something.

So we begin creating our days by the thoughts we have in the morning. Like most people, it is likely that you have spent more time thinking about problems, worries and what needs to be done, although you will also have thought about some things that have felt good. With this mixture of good and bad feeling thoughts, you have given off a mixture of vibrational signals, and you have attracted a mixture of results into your life; many of which you don't like and don't feel so good.

To get a good life, to improve our life and then get an amazing life, we need to realise the importance of what we think about, and what we give our attention to. We need to understand that our thoughts create a vibrational signal that attracts other thoughts, things and situations into our experience.

Think Your Way to Feeling Good

Once you understand that your thoughts and what you give your attention to are dictating how you feel, you have a most powerful insight. You have the power to get more of what is most important to you: you have the power to feel good - and nothing is more important to you than you feel good. With this understanding, all you need to do is to make it a priority that you feel good and decide to think in a way that makes you feel good.

You can do this by acknowledging when good things are happening and when things go your way. Start with simple things and don't undervalue them. So when you get a green traffic light think to yourself, that things are going your way. This may seem simple and even silly, and yet sometimes you find it quite normal to get frustrated and even start yelling at a red light! Appreciate when the traffic is flowing, if you get a perfect parking place or even if someone is kind to you. Take every opportunity to think and feel that life is good and that things are going your way.

The easiest way to have thoughts that feel good, is to appreciate the beauty around you, such as a blue sky, plants, trees, the sun and even the rain. Appreciate anything that makes you feel good: a TV programme you like, something that makes you laugh or someone passes you a compliment. Use any excuse to feel good. Decide to have more thoughts that feel good to you. By doing this, you will be able to feel better more of the time and you will be in the process of creating a life that feels really good.

Having the belief that life is supposed to be good for you means that you are worthy of a good life and you deserve a good life. This does not mean you can have a good life if you work hard. It means you deserve a good life and your life can be the way you want it to be. You don't have to justify your desires to anyone: if you have a desire for something that is justification enough.

Your beliefs are very powerful and a belief is just a thought you keep thinking. So as you keep thinking and believing that life is supposed to be good for you, you will start to see evidence of why life is good. As you look around, you will start to see many reasons why life is already good for you.

You Can Live Your Dream

As was discussed earlier, the universe is not random, but there is an infinite intelligence behind the perfection of the universe. Everything, including your life, has been created for the purpose of joy and happiness. There is no way that an infinite intelligence, with a desire and a plan to create such an amazing and beautiful world, would allow us to have desires and dreams that we could not fulfil, and so lead us to lives of frustration and hopelessness. It defies logic for us to have such strong desires for so many things we cannot have!

Life has been designed to be good for you and that is why there are so many good things to desire. Everything in the universe, including your life, has been created by the infinite intelligence of the universe. It follows that if life has inspired desires and dreams within you, then this infinite intelligence must have the desire, ability and resources to make your desires and dreams a reality.

Many of your dreams and desires for a better life may have been inspired by the lives of other people; perhaps people you admire or people who are famous or successful in some way. These people may have had an advantageous start in life or a special talent, but just as they created what they wanted, you have the power to create your life the way you want it. These people may have created an amazing life because they are a great musician, actor or sports person; yet they are still human beings, the same as you, and their life has been created by the same laws of the universe that are creating your life.

The universe was created by the law of attraction and with mathematical perfection; and your life is created through the same consistent law. People's lives are not random and either lucky or unlucky. Your life and those of the people you admire, are created by thoughts, beliefs and the law of attraction. Just as some lives may seem amazing, so can yours.

Chapter 7

Your Life Can Be Amazing if You Can Believe it

You can create the life you want, but you need to believe it. You have to have that expectation. Everyone that has been successful has expected the best for themselves. They have expected and believed that success was theirs for the taking. There are many stories of successful people who fell into failure, as they lost belief in themselves. Later they found self-belief again and became successful once more.

If you believe that your life can be the way you want it, you will think in a way that attracts more thoughts that support that belief. In the same way, if you believe you probably won't get what you want, you will attract more thoughts about why you will not get what you want. Before long, you can become pretty certain that you will not get what you want.

You can if you believe you can, so don't start with massive goals and dreams that you don't really believe. If you think something would be too good to be true, then you are thinking and saying to the universe that you don't believe it can happen. We need to build up to believing our bigger desires and dreams.

If you can believe that life is supposed to be good for you, it is easy to believe that wonderful things are possible. If you think about things that you really appreciate, enjoy and feel good about, then you are giving off a good feeling vibration. Then by the law of attraction, you will attract more experiences and evidence that show you that your life is already good. Then the thought that your life can get even better will be easy to believe. The more you do this, the easier it will be to have a wonderful vision of the life you really want. And you might even be able to believe it!

Life is meant to be good for you and you can be, do or have whatever you want; if you can believe it. Whether you believe it or not is important because your beliefs are a way of thinking, and it is your thoughts that the law of attraction is responding to. So if you believe your life will not be amazing, then you get what you believe - a life that is not amazing. If you can believe that your life can be amazing, you will have the universe on your side and then anything is possible.

Things Are Working Out for You

The universe knows everything that you want. You have thought it and infinite intelligence is aware of every thought and is responding through the law of attraction. Infinite intelligence takes into consideration all of your desires, in all areas of your life, and law of attraction responds to the vibration of what you are thinking and feeling. Everything is brought to you in perfect response to your vibration and with perfect timing.

Perfect timing means that infinite intelligence is perfectly orchestrating the circumstances of your life, making the best of any situation, in order to best fulfil your desires and dreams. But you are not a puppet on a string! You are in charge of attracting everything into your experience by the power of your thought in accordance with the universal law of attraction. So it is possible that your vibration, your thinking and how you feel can delay or prevent the accomplishment of your dreams and desires.

Life is supposed to be good for you and no matter what, infinite intelligence is always working things out for you. All you have to do is take care of your vibration by caring about what you think and feel.

Care About How You Feel

When you decide to take more control of how you feel, you will begin to choose more thoughts that make you feel good. At first, you will attract more thoughts and feelings that feel good. As you continue to do this, your power of attracting what you want will get stronger and more consistent. You will find your life changing in positive ways and more things coming into your life that make you feel good. This will come to include money and all the things you desire. Your life will feel better and better. You will find more times when you feel good and some times you will even feel that life is amazing. And it will not stop there, it will continue to get better and better - the law of attraction never stops. The universe is abundant and there is no limit to the joy and riches you can experience in your life. Your life is supposed to be good for you and you can have an amazing life.

Enjoy the Journey

Contrary to popular belief, creating a wonderful life is not about working hard and sacrifice. It is not about striving to get a lot of money so we can finally get the stuff and do the things that will finally make us happy.

Our life is a journey and it is a happy journey that leads to a happy destination. That is why it is about being as happy and feeling as good as we can along the way. Life is not about sacrifice and deprivation now, in the hope of brighter, happier future. Life is about making the best of things and feeling good now; then by law of attraction we will attract more that feels good. Our life gets better and better this way: as we enjoy the journey, it just keeps getting better and better and we end up somewhere we really like. We don't suddenly get to a place in life and finally feel that life is amazing. We notice that life is amazing in a million ways along the way; that is how we find our way to a life that is amazing.

So give yourself the time in the morning to think and appreciate things. Give yourself time to walk in nature when possible in your day. Don't keep busy all the time: life is not all about what you can accomplish and complete. If you are too busy, you rarely take time to have pleasant, good-feeling thoughts. You don't really find things to appreciate and you don't really feel good too often. If you are too busy, you are more likely to be stressed and anxious. As you think and feel this way, you attract more stressful thoughts. If you continue with this train of thought, you will attract even more stressful situations. The busier you are, the less time you have and feeling good feels like a luxury you can't afford. When your focus is a to-do list, you can only imagine feeling good when you get everything done. But there is a flaw in this thinking - you never get it all done, there is always something else. This is just the law of attraction showing you, you always get more of what you think about.

Life is an emotional experience and everything you do, is in the hope that you will feel better. So if you want your life to improve, make it is a priority to feel good: begin your day that way, and find times in your day to be grateful, appreciate things and feel good. Give yourself time to relax more. Take time to laugh more. Do things that you like more. Treat yourself well, be kind to yourself and tell yourself that life is supposed to be good for you. The time you give yourself to feel good is the most important time of your life.

Now go easy on all this as you strive to feel better and make your life better. You have habits of thought that you have picked up and practised throughout your life. Go easy on yourself and don't try to change everything all at once. Take your time, and at first, just feel good that you now have more clarity and you know the direction you want your life to take. Enjoy the process of building your life the way you want it to be by the way you think and feel. Enjoy creating and being in a great mood but don't worry when you don't feel in a good mood. You are heading in the right direction, and the way you feel will get better and better more of the time. The life you have so far created out of a lifetime of mixed thoughts, worry, frustration and confusion, will slowly but surely evolve and improve. You can sit back and take delight in each small improvement that you see, as you move towards the brilliant, beautiful life you have already created in your dreams.

The Most Important Hour of Your Life

Set aside time each day when your focus is to feel good. Remember, the better you feel about life, the more good you are attracting into your life. So give yourself the time and make it a priority to think thoughts that get you in a good mood - whatever works for you. You might feel grateful for parts of your life and the people in your life. You might feel good appreciating the amazing beautiful world we live in. You could acknowledge and appreciate the perfect design of the earth. Considering the infinite intelligence behind the creation of life and the world in which we live might feel good to you. It might be inspiring to remember that everything is designed for you to have a great and amazing life. You could think that infinite intelligence is on your side and wants you to have a great life.

You have the freedom and power to create the life you want. You can decide to feel empowered and believe in how wonderful and amazing your life can be. You can decide to give yourself this time out of the busy-ness, stress and demands of your daily life for what is most important to you. You could decide to take time to consider that just as our beautiful earth and universe was created by the law of attraction, so you can make your life beautiful and abundant by the thoughts you think, what you believe and how you feel.

This could be the most important hour of your life: you can read this book in an hour or two and gain the most important, amazing insight and understanding. This could then lead you to everything that is most important to you. But it is not just the time to read this book that is so important; it is the time you give yourself everyday to create the life you want. What could be more important than that?

The most important hour may not be a literal hour in the day, but an amount of time throughout your day, when you are thinking in a way and doing things that help to create your good mood. Perhaps your most important hour could include time reading something inspiring, listening to music you love, meditating, walking in nature or just relaxing.

When you have this time, you don't go over problems and try to find solutions. This will just pull your mood down. You find the best solutions to your problems when you are feeling good. When you are feeling better, your intelligence is higher and your inner wisdom is more accessible. So if you need to, look at your problems briefly later, when your mood is higher.

Your most important hour could be a time to relax, feel good and treat yourself well. This might feel a little selfish, as we may have grown up being told that it is more important to think of others before ourselves; to be good to others and forget ourselves. Yet you need to give yourself this most important time first. When you are feeling good, when you are in control of your life, when you are in a good mood, you naturally want to help other people anyway. You want to do things for other people, but it is not at the expense of yourself. When you feel good about yourself and your life, then you really have something to offer. You can't help others to be happy when you are not happy. You cannot find love and patience for others when you are not first loving and patient with yourself.

Allow Yourself to be Amazed

This world in which we live has been created with such precision, abundance and beauty - it is incredible. The earth has been spinning in perfect proximity to the sun. The sun has been giving off its heat and light and beautiful sunsets for us to enjoy everyday. So much beauty, harmony and the perfect conditions for life on earth have been maintained in perfection for billions of years.

Yet there is even more going on than maintaining this perfect balance and harmony of life on earth. The universe is still expanding, earth has been evolving and life on earth has been getting better and better. Firstly, earth evolved from a cloud of gas and dust to form a spinning sphere of rock. From here the evolution continued to create a most beautiful planet, of vibrant blue waters and ideal atmosphere: the perfect conditions for life. A planet unique in our known universe.

Earth continued its evolution, as it gave birth to life. Life on earth evolved and eventually, humanity was born into the most beautiful, fertile, abundant and perfect environment for life. Conditions so perfect that humanity and all life has not only survived, but thrived. Humanity developed the perfect physical and mental abilities, not just to survive on earth, but to be able to see, hear, touch, taste and smell, all the beauty and abundance the earth has to offer. Evolution still continues to this day with the evolution of human civilisations. Our civilisations have developed infrastructure, transport, and built amazing architecture. There have been continual creative developments in art, music and entertainment. Science and technology has evolved and improved our world beyond the dreams of our ancestors. And the development and evolution of life continues to this day. Just as the universe is still expanding, so is our life on earth.

Take a moment to comprehend the brilliance of the universe and life on earth. Consider the existence of the invisible infinite intelligence that has made all this possible. Remember the only rational reason and purpose for life is for it to be good and get even better. The purpose of your life is joy and happiness. Life is meant to be good for you and with this understanding you are on the path to making your life better and better.

Of course, on this brief journey through our history, there are many undesirable events and situations that I could have mentioned, from the ice age and earthquakes to the world wars, starvation and crime etc. but none of these events have halted the evolution of life on earth. In fact, out of each catastrophic event or undesirable situation, the world has emerged a better place. The ice age allowed life to evolve beyond the dinosaurs and the world wars inspired greater desire and determination for peace and international cooperation. Through the contrasting experiences of what we do not want, we clarify what we do want, we move towards what we want and continue our evolution.

We can always look at the undesirable things in history and in our own lives but there is much more that is good than bad. We give our attention to the good things in life because we want our life to be full of good things. We don't change the world or our lives for the better, by giving our attention to all that we don't want. We change the world by changing our own world.

As you make your life the way you want it, you will bring much more happiness, love and peace into your own life and into the world. There is nothing more important than you make your life amazing and wonderful; and you can do that everyday by being aware of what you are thinking and deciding that nothing is more important than you feel good. Do this and enjoy watching your life get better and better. Life is supposed to be good for you and your life can be amazing.

Chapter 8

The Most Important Hour of
Your Life

To make your life amazing you need time for yourself and you need to be able to take control of how you feel. As you begin to think in a certain way, you will begin to feel better and attract more of the things you want into your life.

Until now, you probably have not known the power that you have to create the life you want. Life is meant to be good for you and there is a never-ending flow of positive energy, health, well-being and abundance flowing to you every moment of every day. The question is, are you allowing it into your life?

When you feel good, when you feel happy, when you are having fun, when you feel relaxed, when you are care-free, when you are appreciating something, when you feel grateful, when you feel love - you are allowing good energy to flow and you are a beacon attracting into your life more of what will make you feel good.

So you might say, 'If there is all this positive energy and law of attraction bringing everything to me, then why isn't my life better than this?' The answer is that although we do have times when we feel good, there is a lot of time when we don't feel that good. Often we find ourselves worrying about something; we worry that things won't turn out the way we want them to; we feel frustrated with things; we criticise and we complain. We have lots of things that we think about that don't make us feel good. We probably spend much more time feeling busy, stressed or overwhelmed. We might be reacting to and thinking about how others have treated us or we might be thinking about any number of problems we have. We are so good at thinking about things that are not going well or that don't feel good and the older we get the more we do it. Our time of ease and going with the flow of life seems to be reserved for holidays or certain times when we go out with friends; the rest of our life can feel pretty hard going.

To make our lives better and to feel better more of the time, we need to prioritise feeling good. We need to decide that it is most important for us to feel good. Only then can we begin to allow the wonders of life to flow into our experience. When we do this, we are on the path to creating a life that will feel amazing.

Here are some suggestions of activities that can help you feel good and allow positive energy to flow to you, so that you can begin to attract all you want in life. Your life is a journey and here is how you can make it the most fun, enjoyable and amazing journey ever. Have fun with this and don't take anything too seriously.

Care About How You Feel

Make it a priority that you feel good. Remember that there is nothing more important than you feel good and that it is your thinking that makes you feel the way you do. If you are feeling good, it is a sign that you are thinking in away that is allowing positive energy to flow to you and through you.

Decide to care about what you think about and what you give your attention to. Be aware of how you feel and let your emotions be your guide. Your emotions tell you what you are thinking, what vibe you are giving off and what you are attracting.

Decide to give yourself time in the morning and throughout your day to do some of the activities suggested here. Choose what you do by how it feels.

If the idea of something feels good to you, then give that a try.

Start Your Day in the Right Way

When you consider the law of attraction, you realise how important it is to start the day in the right way. If you start with thoughts that feel good, you can attract more that feels good and you will find it easier to maintain a good feeling. Your day will go smoother, as more things respond to your good feeling vibration; you will begin to notice more things working out for you; you will find yourself being more positive and you will notice more things around you that you can feel good about.

Start your day with a way of thinking and activity that works for you and feels good. As you wake and relax before getting out of bed be sure that your thoughts are about things you can appreciate and be grateful for. Perhaps enjoy your bed for a moment longer, the soft pillow and cosy covers and how perfectly comfortable you feel. As you step out of bed, think of things that you can be grateful for and that you can appreciate. Appreciate that you had a great sleep. Feel grateful that you have warm clothes to wear or appreciate a refreshing shower. You can even enjoy and appreciate the fragrance of the shower gel and the refreshing sensation of hot water on your skin. The possibilities are endless; you discover what you can think about that feels good.

Your morning schedule should include time to start your day in a way that feels good. You could drink and eat something nice while you find things to appreciate and be grateful for. You could include time for 15 minutes meditation or getting outside for a walk.

Avoid problems and worrisome thoughts whenever possible. Watching the breakfast news gives away your thoughts to anything bad that is happening - good news is rarely reported. So keep control of your own thinking in the morning especially. In doing so, you set up your day to attract more things that you like and that will feel good.

Meditation

There is nothing strange or difficult about meditation. If it sounds strange or unusual, you don't even need to call it meditation, just think of it as a bit of quiet time where you stop the chatter of your mind. It is simply giving yourself the opportunity to take control of your thinking, so that you can slow the momentum of any negative thoughts and allow yourself to get in tune with your natural well-being. This is very simple activity, except that for most of us it doesn't feel natural to keep still for more than 2 minutes. This very problem was addressed by Charles Haanel in *The Master Key System* (1919) where he guides the reader patiently over the course of a number of weeks to experience the benefit of meditation by first encouraging a time of just sitting quietly and building up to some guided visualisation and meditation exercises. We normally only keep still and quiet when we are either asleep or watching television. We have probably not been giving ourselves time to stop the stress of all our thinking because we have not known that so much of our thinking has been having a negative impact on our experience.

The benefits of meditation are that you are able to relax, quiet your mind and allow yourself to connect to your natural state of well-being. As you allow your mind to slow down, you give yourself the opportunity to release troubling thoughts that make you feel stressed. By not thinking about your problems and concerns you allow your vibration to rise. Your natural state, without worry and stress, is one of health, vitality and feeling good. When you are in this state, you are not only feeling better but your vibration and what you are attracting into your life is so much better.

Meditation is very simple: it is essentially just relaxing your mind and body. All you need to do is sit comfortably where you will not be disturbed for perhaps 15 or 20 minutes. You can also lie down, although you might find that you fall asleep. Then when you are comfortable, close your eyes and relax by focusing on your breathing. Some people prefer a silent room, whereas some people like to have gentle instrumental music in the background. As you try it you can find a way of meditation that suites you.

If you have any troubling thoughts as you begin your meditation, just try to keep putting your attention back on your breathing. Relaxing your mind may feel difficult at first, as you may not be used to it. We are used to constant ways to occupy our mind and we rarely have a quiet mind; even if we have a quiet minute, we have a quick look at our phone. We might even 'relax' by looking at our phone before we go to sleep at night!

There is no need to make a big effort to meditate. If it feels like effort, then you are probably not going to find it very enjoyable or helpful. It may be that at this time a walk might feel more relaxing to you. Its all about how you feel and nothing is more important than you feel good. So let how you feel decide what is right for you.

Appreciation, Gratitude and Love

You get what you think about; so you can tell how you have been thinking by how you are feeling. If you choose thoughts of appreciation, gratitude and love during your day, you will feel good more of the time. Consider everything around you and notice what there is that you can appreciate. Wherever you are you can find things that feel good or that you can appreciate or be grateful for; everything from a hot shower to your mobile phone can be appreciated.

Allow yourself to think appreciative thoughts about anything that you like.

If you are outside find aspects of nature and the weather to appreciate. It is easy to find things to be grateful for and yet it is just as easy to overlook them. So don't miss the opportunity to feel grateful, for it could be in that moment of gratitude that you feel wonderful; even if it is only for a moment.

It is not only about feeling gratitude for the big things, like a lovely birthday present or a new car. You can find feelings of gratitude when someone is nice to you or you find something that makes you smile. You can appreciate the warmth of the sun, the comfort of your home, the fun you share with friends or a nice cup of coffee. Whatever you like, and whatever makes you feel good, take a moment to acknowledge and enjoy that good feeling.

Thinking about what and who you love is obviously a great way to feel good. Those you love and those who love you can bring you so much good feeling just by thinking about them.

Love could be defined as a profound appreciation and a desire to be with or have that which we love. We feel love for so many things and the richness of our lives is made of all the things and people we feel love for. We can feel love for other people, ourselves, our pets, for life and for the world in which we live. When we appreciate in this way, we cannot help but feel profound gratitude for all we have and we feel the richness of our lives.

We can feel wonderful in the moment we think in this way and when we do we are attracting more wonderful things to come our way.

Positive Aspects

In every moment of every day there are things that we like and things that we don't like. There are aspects of every person and each situation we encounter that we like and other aspects that we don't like. When we give our attention to the things that we like we feel good; however we often find ourselves noticing and giving most of our attention to what annoys us or what we disagree with. As we focus on these aspects that we consider negative, we don't feel good.

We have become experts at finding what we consider wrong. We are quick to discuss the negative aspects of the news and the mistakes and misfortunes of the rich and famous. The worse something is, the more likely we are to talk about it and emphasise how bad it is.

As we consider the negative aspects of people and situations, we are heading in the opposite direction of feeling good. Instead of feeling good, we are attracting feelings of distain, criticism, frustration and even anger. You may not have considered this previously, but these negative thoughts and feelings don't feel that good. Compare this to the feelings of appreciation, happiness, fun and joy that you experience when you are looking at something that you really like.

The point is that we are always choosing what we give our attention to and this determines how we feel. If you are able to practice giving your attention to the aspects you like about people, situations and your life, you will feel better more of the time.

Now this sounds simple but it might not be easy at first. This is because you and all the people around you have habits of thought: we are all well practised at criticising, complaining and thinking about the negative aspects of things. Not only that, there are many aspects of our society and culture that has a more negative bias. Look at how the news is focused on all the negative, violent, criminal and depressing events and situations. The most terrible things form all over the world are dramatised to music and streamed into our living rooms and onto our mobile phones. It is no wonder that we feel our life and the world is so dangerous and miserable much of the time.

Yet no matter what the news is reporting or what other people talk about and believe, we are the ones who create our own experience of life by what we give our attention to, the way we think and how we feel. The good news is that we can choose to watch the news or not. We can decide to find what's wrong or we can focus on what is going well. We can use our time and the power of our mind to create the life we want or we can contemplate misery and suffering.

Why should we think about all the terrible things in the world? The popular answer is that we need to know about all the bad things so that we can avoid them. In a similar way, parents tell their children every possible danger, in the hope that this will help to keep them safe. This is understandable and is an expression of how much parents love and care for their children and desire so much for their safety and wellbeing. And yet this amplification and emphasis of the negative aspects of life is made without knowledge of the law of attraction and without understanding that we create our own reality.

The more we think about danger, illness and suffering, the worse we feel. As we do this we will attract more thoughts and feelings of our vulnerability and feel that something bad might happen at any time. As we think this way more and more, our thoughts become beliefs. We believe that the world is a dangerous place and we don't feel safe a lot of the time. As you think in this way you will attract evidence into your life that proves how vulnerable you are and how dangerous the world is.

On the contrary, if you are able to give your attention and thoughts to what is going well, you will feel good. As you get into the habit of noticing the positive aspects of your life and the world, you will find more and more evidence that shows you how good life is; and you will begin to attract more and more things, people and situations that you can feel good about.

You create your experience of life by the thoughts you think and the way you feel. So if you give your attention and thoughts to the positive aspects of your life; you will feel better and your life will get better and better.

Make the Best of It

Many times in our days we find things don't go the way we want them to and we can feel bad. The more we think about it, the worse we tend to feel. If you are not able to find something to feel good about, your negative thinking will gain momentum and pretty soon you find that you cannot stop thinking about what is troubling you. This could be the beginning of a bad day, unless you can get your mind off your troubles and onto something that feels better.

The sooner you are able to find something that feels better to think about, the easier it will be to prevent your thinking slipping into a downward spiral. There are always things that we can feel good about or grateful for; after all, we were probably feeling fine before this thing went wrong.

Sometimes you can find a positive within the situation that didn't go the way you wanted it to. At other times it is best to take your mind off the negative as soon as possible; and usually the only way you can do this is to put your mind on something else. Think about something else in your life that you like or that is going well. This is a lot easier when you have some powerful positive beliefs such as: things usually work out, things are never as bad as they usually seem, life is good for me, life is supposed to be good for me and I create my own reality by the way I think.

Once you begin to see that you can have a lot more control over the way you think and therefore how you feel, you will feel more in control and find it easier to make the best of any situation. Even if you cannot feel good straightaway, you will find that you have the ability to recover and feel better much quicker than ever before.

Imagination

Our imagination is a powerful and wonderful thing. We have the ability to create anything and everything in our mind: the power and creativity of our imagination is limitless. Through our imagination our thoughts come to life: we can create wonderful images and even movies in our mind.

"Imagination is more important than knowledge. For knowledge is limited to all we now know and understand, while imagination embraces the entire world, and all there ever will be to know and understand"

Albert Einstein

Just like our thinking, our imagination has the power to make us feel wonderful or terrible depending how we use it. In the past we have probably used our imagination to re-live past unpleasant experiences or to worry and imagine how things could go wrong. However, now you know the power your thinking has to shape your life, you can appreciate how important it is to use your imagination to feel good.

In our imagination we can decide what we think and so we can choose to dream, fantasise, remember and create whatever we want. The only thing for us to make sure is that what we have in our mind is making us feel good. Then we can enjoy the wonder of our imagination and see how good we can feel. The point here is to show how valuable our imagination is in helping us to feel good.

We know that there is nothing more important to us than we feel good but how have we been trying to feel good so far? Usually, when we want to feel good our first thought is, what can I do? And by this we usually mean a physical action or activity. Yet through our imagination we have access to feeling good without doing anything or going anywhere.

Take time, say 15 minutes to enjoy your imagination and see how good you can feel. You could sit somewhere quiet, in bed, in the car or anywhere. Then simply think of anything that makes you feel good. Picture yourself doing something, being somewhere or with someone where you feel happy, excited, full of fun, passionate or any way that feels go to you. This is a great opportunity to imagine how you would like your future to be. The clearer you are about how you want your life to be, the more power you have to attract it into your experience. Although it is not the details of your vision that has the most power to attract, it is how good you feel. As you feel good, you attract more things that make you feel that way.

You could think about and imagine anything you do now that feels good. What would you do today if you could do anything you wanted to? Think about these things and imagine the feeling, hear the sounds, see the colours and feel the sensations that feel so good.

Then imagine anything you would love to do in the future. Picture the things, the people and the circumstances that would feel wonderful and that would make your life amazing. Don't limit your imagination to what you consider realistic - the purpose of this exercise is to use your mind and your thoughts to make you feel really good and think about whatever you would really like your life to be like. How would you love to feel and what would make you feel that way? What are your most brilliant dreams?

The more time you spend feeling good, the stronger you are attracting more good things into your life and the closer you are getting to the amazing life that you have seen in your dreams.

Your Hour of Power

A number of years ago, I was inspired to give myself time in the morning or evening, where I would walk or run and think in a way that made me feel good. The 'hour of power' was a process that was presented by Anthony Robbins in his audio programme *Get the Edge*. I enjoyed following his audio description of this process and then took from the process the parts that felt good to me.

I would set off walking and taking deep breaths, as I enjoyed the fresh air. After a few minutes, I felt quite energised and I then began to think about anything that I felt like being grateful for. I sometimes began with grateful thoughts about my family and other times I just felt like appreciating nature. Sometimes it just felt good that I had this time to myself and at other times I appreciated my body and my health. After 5 minutes or so of thinking like this I felt noticeably better about life: I felt various combinations of positive good feelings, such as appreciation, gratitude, inspiration, freedom and contentment.

As I developed this into an almost daily habit, I was able to control my thinking so that this was a time free from thoughts about work, problems or things I had to do. It was my time to connect to a most wonderful feeling.

After a short time thinking thoughts of gratitude and appreciation, I then began to think about how wonderful I would like my life to be. It was fun and quite exciting to allow myself to visualise how I wanted my life to be. It was fun because I believed that visualising the life I wanted was in fact bringing it closer to me. If I thought my thoughts had no power to affect my future, it would not have been so much fun. Yet I did feel I was helping to create my future by my thoughts and imagination. It was so much fun visualising myself in a beautiful home and having a fabulous holiday. I also imagined having fun in the future and tried to imagine and create that feeling in my mind. I thought about how I would feel wearing nice clothes, how I would feel driving a nice car and even the sound of the gravel as I drove up the driveway of my beautiful home. I imagined feeling so healthy and enjoyed thinking how it would feel to laugh and have fun with friends. Once again I found this developed such a wonderful, inspired and optimistic feeling within me. This became such an important hour for me. Even if I only had half an hour, I always looked forward to it and felt better every time.

To this day, I enjoy this time so much that I still make time for my 'hour of power'. Even when I am on holiday with my family, I find it invaluable to take the time for myself. It is such an energising and fulfilling time because there is so much to appreciate and be grateful for: being on holiday with the people I love, the beauty of the palm trees, the blue sky, the delicious heat of the sun, the warm ocean breeze; and that is just the beginning. I then think of the nice times I can look forward to later in my day and all the fun I plan to have. As I walk in the heat of the day I sometimes feel like running and then I appreciate the power and fitness of my body. I sometimes discover a new beautiful view and I stop to take it all in. It is a time of bliss and pure enjoyment.

This is a wonderful process. Why not give yourself this most important time? What could you be grateful for and feel good about? How would your life look like if you could have it any way you wanted? What would you be doing? What would you be wearing? Where would you be living? Who would you be with? Just enjoy this process, have fun with it and enjoy how it makes you feel. Have fun with your imagination; it is very powerful. As you think in this way and feel good, you are affecting your vibration and actually attracting wonderful things into your experience.

Inspiration

Life is a great teacher: be aware of life offering inspirations and insight to you. Remember, there is a universal intelligence that knows your thoughts and dreams, life is supposed to be good for you and your life is meant to get better and better. As you think and feel this way, you will attract many inspirations and insights: thoughts and ideas will just pop into your mind. As you consider your dreams and what you want in life, you will attract thoughts, ideas and impulses to help you on your way to the fulfilment of your desires.

You might get an impulse or inspiration to read a particular book or to watch a certain movie. If you decide to watch a movie you might receive inspiration from the movie or it might make you think about something in a new way. The movie might make you feel good and that in itself is a wonderful thing. After all, nothing is more important than you feel good!

Let Your Emotions be Your Guide

We are faced with choices everyday and sometimes we try to weigh the pros and cons in order to make a decision; and yet decisions are still sometimes difficult to make. Remember that more than anything you want to feel good and everything we do, is in the hope that we will feel better. It follows that considering how we feel is the most important factor in deciding anything. So when deciding anything, first decide how you want to feel.

You have a very simple, yet very powerful guidance system. When you are feeling good you are on the right track. When you are not feeling good you are a little off track from what you want. When you understand this you can see that all you have to do is to decide that you want to feel better. When you decide that you want to feel better, you will get the idea or inspiration of how you can feel better. You may see clearly the way you want things to be or something you want to do. If you follow your own guidance, you will see how easy it is to make decisions based upon what makes you feel good.

Remember, life is supposed to be good for you and universal intelligence in on your side. Some may say that this is a very selfish way to run your life but you have to be this way since it is only you who creates your reality: it is your thoughts and feelings that are creating your life. People may not like you having this control of your life because often other people want you to do what makes them feel good. They want you to act according to their thoughts, beliefs and what makes them feel good. It is your life, so you first of all decide what you want out of your life and then let your emotions be your guide.

Emotions may seem quite varied and complicated, but there is a much easier way to understand them. Your emotions are simply how you feel and there are only two types of feelings: those that feel good and those that feel bad. When you are feeling good you are on the right path: the path to getting what you want. When you feel bad, your emotions are showing you that you are thinking in a way that is depriving you of what you really want.

Do you remember playing the hot and cold game where someone hid something and then you had to find it? As you looked for what was hidden you were told you were either getting hotter or colder. As you got closer, you were told you were getting hotter. If you went the wrong way, you were getting colder. With these simple clues you found what you were looking for every time. And this is how it is with your emotional guidance. When you are getting closer to what you want you feel good, when you are heading further away from what you want, you don't feel so good.

The very core of you wants to feel good because the essence of who you are knows that you are good and that life is supposed to feel good. Therefore your emotional guidance is always telling you whether you are feeling good or not. In this way, you have the perfect compass pointing you in the direction of what feels good and what you really want.

Everything we do and everything we want is because we want to feel good and we think or hope that we will feel better when we get or do the thing we want. Since what is most important to us is how we feel, we should first decide how we want to feel before we do anything. When we know how we want to feel, we can decide how we want things to be or what we want to have so that we can feel the way we want to feel.

This is very good as a written exercise. You can take a minute or two to write down how you want to feel. For example, you might write, I want to be happy, I want to feel excited, I want to feel fun, I want to feel confident, I want to feel enjoyment, passion, enthusiasm, etc. Once you have done this you can spend 5 minutes or so writing down what you would like to have or the way you want things to be, so that you can feel the way you have described. For example, you might decide you want to feel really happy. As you consider this you can ask yourself what would give you this feeling. As you do this you could get an image in your mind of laughing and having fun. Now you are clearer what you want. Now you know what you want, you can decide what to do to get what you want. In this case you could give your friends a call and get something arranged.

When you are deciding with your friends what to do, remember you really want to have fun. This will affect what you decide to do. Knowing in advance how you want to feel will even affect which friends you decide to call. Some friends are quieter, which you like sometimes and other friends are usually full of energy and good for a laugh. In this way, by putting how you feel first you are much more likely to get what you want.

Tomorrow is a New Beginning

Each new day is the best opportunity to start to feel good again. The morning is the time we begin a new momentum of thinking and this determines how we feel. This also begins attracting similar thoughts and feelings that often set the tone for our day.

If we begin our day remembering bad events of the previous days, we set ourselves up for another day of not feeling good. So get into the habit of finding thoughts that feel good as soon as you wake up. Think about things that are going well or what you can be grateful for.

Nothing is more important than you feel good and the morning is the best time to kick-start your thinking in a way that feels good. Then by the law of attraction, you will attract similar thoughts that feel good and the momentum of your thinking will grow in a way that feels good. In this way, you begin shaping your day with the thoughts you have from the time you wake up.

There will be times when you don't feel things are going well for you and you are having a bad day. When you are feeling bad, you can't suddenly think positive. Often the best you can do is to distract yourself by doing something to take your mind off what is making you feel bad and ride out the storm of bad feelings. When things do feel bad, it is good to know that you can start again tomorrow and you will be in a better position to think about things that feel good. You don't have to try to work things out when you are feeling bad. Have a good sleep and try again in the morning.

Have Fun

There is nothing more important than you feel good and life is supposed to be good for you. So it is up to you to decide to have fun and do things that feel good to you. What would be fun for you? What do you enjoy doing? What makes you feel really good? Make feeling good a priority and make time to do the things you love: this is some of the most important time of your life.

The Most Important Hour

The most important hour of your life is the time you give yourself to feel as good as you can. It is a time you give yourself to make your life feel wonderful. Incorporate any of these ideas and activities that feel good to you into your life and find things to enjoy everyday. You will start to notice your life getting better and better in small ways at first. You will start to think a little more positively and start to feel better more of the time. In time, you will have bigger and better changes in your life and before you know it, you will be able to see that your life is in fact wonderful in many ways. You can make your life amazing and what you have here is a recipe for an amazing life.

Chapter 9

A Matter of Life and Death

Life on earth is wonderful, with so much to appreciate and enjoy and this is just part of the amazing universe created by universal intelligence. Our purpose in being here is to follow our bliss and to seek joy and fun in a million different ways. We have a lifetime to explore and enjoy this amazing world with our wonderful sensitive bodies and brilliant minds. Not only that, we are able to attract into our lives whatever we want by the power of our thoughts and the law of attraction because life has been designed to be so good for us by the universal intelligence that is the origin of the universe. Life is supposed to be so good for us and even get better and better. For this reason the last chapter of this book describes how we can even live happily ever after. However in my desire to express how wonderful this physical life can be and how much there is to appreciate in the physical world, I have discussed very little about illness and disease, suffering and death. So before the happy ending I have planned I feel it is important to shed a little light on these difficult but most important aspects of life; and so before we progress to living happily ever after let us look briefly at why life may not be so happy and what is the meaning of illness, disease and death.

If we believe that life is random and uncertain, it is very difficult for us to believe that we can look forward to a life filled with happiness, where things keep working out for us. We are more likely to just hope for the best but feeling that things could all go wrong. There are examples all around us and perhaps even in our own lives, where life has delivered some very unpleasant surprises and situations. Without an understanding of the vibrational nature of the universe, the law of attraction and how we create our own reality, it is logical for us to believe that ill-health, financial difficulty or a broken heart could be just around the corner; and the older we get, we feel justified in believing that ill-health and physical deterioration is an even bigger threat. When we think about things in this way it feels impossible to believe in a happy life that just keeps getting better and better.

We can only truly believe in happy life, a life in which our dreams come true and where life keeps getting better, when we believe that life is supposed to be good for us and that the invisible powers of the universe are on our side. It is only by having new beliefs about life to replace our old fearful beliefs that we can have hope and belief in our life becoming the way we want it to be.

Our old beliefs about illness, for example, might tell us that illness and disease could spring upon anyone at any time or that a certain disease or medical condition has been inherited and is in our genes. However this relies on an assumption that we are at the mercy of the world around us and does not take into account that we are powerful beings who attract everything that comes to us. These old beliefs or ways of thinking do not consider that we create our own reality and that we have the power to do this by the thoughts we think and the beliefs we hold.

As Dr. Bruce Lipton explains in his groundbreaking work in the field of genetics: it is your thoughts and beliefs that determine the health of your body not your genes or DNA.

"It is not our genes but our beliefs that control our lives..."

"The moment you change your perception is the moment you rewrite the chemistry of your body"

When we hold empowering beliefs about life that tell us that life is supposed to be good for us and that we create our own reality, then we can come to feel more in control of our future and our destiny. We can come to feel as the English poet William Ernest Henley wrote"

"I am the master of my fate, I am the captain of my soul."

When we are young we don't tend to think about disease and old age as it doesn't seem to apply to us. Yet as we get older we eventually begin to think about this as we witness our bodies and those around us getting older. We might observe some things happening that we don't want or that feel unpleasant: more wrinkles, grey hair, hair loss, loss of physical strength and increased chances of illness and disease such as cancer and dementia. This doesn't paint a pretty picture of our future; how on earth can we imagine looking forward to living happily if we have this to look forward to? And this is without considering the biggest thing we have to look forward to - death! Yes, we are all going to die at some point and this doesn't fill many people with a sense of joy and happiness.

It seems that I have just brought up everything that will prevent us from feeling good rather than helping us to believe that life is supposed to be good for us. Well things don't look so good when we look at life and death with the prevailing beliefs of our society and culture.

For us to be able to live happily we need to have a new understanding and some new beliefs about life, illness and death. These are very big topics to discuss and are certainly important to us all. I will discuss these topics briefly here but probably not in enough detail to answer many of the questions you may have.

So far I have attempted to explain how life can be good for you and that life is beautiful, wonderful and can get better and better for you. Yet how can we think of living happily in life when there is the grim prospect of death on the horizon for all of us? Well like everything we have discussed so far, it depends on how you think about it. What if death is not bad? What if we are much more than the physical self that we call me or I? Most people would agree that we are more than just physical: we have mind, consciousness, feelings, thought and many would say we have a spirit, soul or higher-self. Most people therefore feel, believe or want to believe that there is more to life than meets the eye.

At this point I would like to point out that we all have our own beliefs about everything and that includes the subject of death and our own mortality. I would also like to remind you that our beliefs are just thoughts that we believe are true. So I would like us to consider what we believe about death. I can explain what I feel is true about life, death and life after death but just like everything else in this book, it is only my way of thinking and what I believe. Yes, I have researched and studied these subjects for over 25 years but I have still made my conclusions based on my thinking and what makes sense to me. In the same way, as you think about what is written here, you will have your own unique perspective; your own unique mixture of thoughts, life experiences and beliefs. All you can do, all any of us can do, is to consider, think and decide what makes sense for ourselves.

I would also like to add that if life is supposed to be good for us then the way we think about life and what we believe about life should feel good. I would like to offer that if life is supposed to be good and it was conceived and created by an infinite intelligence, for the purpose of joy and goodness, then the experience of death is not something to be feared and is not something bad.

At this point, anyone who has experienced the death of a loved one would probably disagree with me but I am speaking from the perspective of those that die and not from the perspective of those still alive in the physical world who feel the profound pain of loss. It is also logical to consider death to be bad when we consider the unpleasant circumstances of many deaths.

Just as our life is our own and we create our own reality so our death is our own and therefore it follows that we are the ones who can decide whether our own death is good or bad. Interestingly, those that die don't seem to see it as a bad experience. But how can I say this? After all, if someone dies they are not around to tell us what it is like? Well, in actual fact, there are many testimonies of people who have died and lived to tell the tale!

In the best-selling book *Life After Life*, psychiatrist Raymond A. Moody describes many accounts of people who had near death experiences: they experienced physical death before being brought back to life. Their testimonies were compelling as they described leaving their bodies and observing all those around them trying to save them or experiencing the pain of loss. The circumstances of each near death were unique and yet when those who almost died later described their unique, and often life-changing experience, they offered striking similarities in their experience.

Those who experienced this near death did not experience any pain or trauma. On the contrary, they all explained an out-of-body experience and an overwhelming wonderful feeling of peace and well-being. They had a feeling of being welcomed by loved ones who had previously died. They had a feeling of being surrounded by a profound feeling of love and even meeting or communicating with a being of light. It was sometimes described as being drawn into a pure white light; something like being immersed into pure liquid love. They expressed an experience of another world; one of profound beauty. They were also allowed the experience of assessing their life experience and then discovering that it was not their time to die. As they realised this they felt great resistance in returning to the physical world as they felt so good where they were.

Overall, the many testimonies of near death experiences can be summarised by saying that the experience of death, for those who die, is a most wonderful experience that is difficult to describe and express in earthly terms. So for the person who dies, it seems that death is good. It is so good that when they are being brought back to life they feel disappointment that they have to leave the profound feeling of love and beauty that they have experienced.

So it seems that death might not be so bad after all - for those who die at least. And this is logical, since this amazing life has been created in all its infinite beauty and wonder by an infinite intelligence; a life that is still evolving and getting better and better. Did the infinite intelligence of the universe just run out of good ideas when the ending to physical life was decided upon? After taking billions of years to create a most amazing beautiful and perfect life on earth does it make sense that a good and beautiful life on earth should end in a painful and ugly death?

No, it only makes sense that just as life is meant to be good for you, death or the end of your physical life, is also meant to be good. And just as the intelligence that is the cause and origin of life is infinite, so it makes sense that life is infinite and that life continues after death. Death is therefore not a permanent end but it is a transition into something even greater.

Does this sound unrealistic and overly optimistic? But isn't this what we want to believe? Isn't this what we would want to tell anyone who has just lost someone they loved? Don't we want to believe that love lasts forever? I do not want to try to convince you of whether this is the truth or not. I want what is best for you and what feels good to you. Therefore I believe what matters is that you believe what makes sense to you and that what you believe about life makes you feel good.

Let's say there is no proof of life after death or that no one knows if there is anything good to look forward to after we die. Well if that is the case and there is no proof either way, we can just choose what we want to believe. So why not believe something that feels good? Just as life is supposed to be good for you, you can believe that after this physical life you have even more wonderful feelings and experiences to look forward to. If you believe this, you are not on your own; the majority of religions and spiritual beliefs that have been held throughout history and around the world, express the idea of life continuing beyond this physical life. The majority of religions that existed before the time of Christianity for example, held beliefs not only of life after death but also a belief in some form of reincarnation and the idea that we have all had lives before this one.

Yet there are many different beliefs or perspectives on reincarnation. Just as there are many religions that teach reincarnation, there are even more unique understandings and misunderstandings with regard to reincarnation. Some people believe that in the next life we could be reborn as an animal, depending on the kind of life we have lived. There are also many who believe that reincarnation and past lives refer to previous human lives.

The important thing to remember is that beliefs are just the way people think and that you choose your own beliefs based on what makes sense to you and feels good to you. Personally, I see how life on earth is continually evolving and getting better. It therefore only makes sense logically that any future lives I may or may not have will be a more evolved human life rather than a drastic regression into the life of an animal.

A fascinating and insightful perspective on past lives is presented by Dr. Brian Weiss, a traditional psychotherapist, in his best selling book *Many Lives Many Masters*. In his book he describes how he was initially astonished and sceptical when one of his patients began recalling past-life experiences that contained remarkable revelations about Dr. Weiss' family and his dead son.

With the vast array of ideas, beliefs, philosophies and religions about life, which one is the right one? Well don't try to find the one truth and the only belief or religion that everyone should believe in. You have the power to create your reality and you do this by choosing the thoughts you think and the beliefs that you hold. Your job is not to decide what is good for everyone else.

Decide that you want to feel good and have beliefs about your life and about death that feel good to you. Consider believing that even though friends or family may have died physically, they have not ceased to exist: they are around somewhere in a beautiful place. A world of love and beauty that is eternal and magnificent. A world that one day, one fabulous day, all of us will find our way to once again. A place where we may feel more at home than during our physical life. We may once again find ourselves united with all those who have died before us and feeling a sense of love and completeness that may have eluded us during life on earth. This has been described throughout history and even experienced by the many people who died, just for a moment and came back to tell of the love, beauty and wonder that awaits us in the continuing life after this physical life on earth.

Does this sound too good to be true? Too unrealistic and dreamy? Well if it sounds good, how wonderful to live with such beliefs that feel so good. You can choose other beliefs about life after death that don't feel so good, the choice is yours. Some may say there is no proof of life after death but if that is true there is also no proof that there isn't life after death. You can choose to think and believe what feels good to you.

So it is possible to believe and think in a way that means we do not have to fear death. And why would we fear death if we felt that we were going to a wonderful place after we die and that we have many lifetimes to look forward to? Well, there is still the feeling of separation form loved ones whether we die or a loved one has died. There is a profound sense of loss and separation that is difficult to come to terms with. Could we ease the pain if we didn't believe that the separation was so final? What if we felt that we are all much more than just physical beings? If we felt that we were fundamentally a non-physical or spiritual being rather than just a physical being and that life continues after we die perhaps the sense of loss would not feel so final.

In fact, it is possible to understand life and death in a way that reduces the feeling of loss even more: what if we could still communicate with those who are no longer physical? There are many testimonies of people receiving communications from those in the non-physical world. By this I am not referring to the descriptions of mystics, such as Emanuel Swedenborg, who offered fascinating accounts of worlds beyond our physical world or spiritual mediums. I am referring to the many accounts of people experiencing the presence of loved ones who have recently died. This might be in the form of an amazing coincidence or seemingly chance orchestration of events that makes someone think of a loved one who has died, in a profound and meaningful way. There are many stories of communications from an invisible dimension: perhaps strong thoughts and feelings that are suddenly felt and even physical signs such as lights flickering for no apparent reason.

We can only allow and experience these communications if our beliefs do not get in the way. Unfortunately, we live in a society that has a system of beliefs that predominantly makes everything that is not physical scary, fearful and possibly dangerous. By this we are saying in our mind that we want nothing to do with those who have died. Just as we live in fear of so many things in life, we have even more fear of death and all that lies after death.

As a society and a culture we perpetuate this fear and we torture ourselves as we create horror stories and movies of evil, ghosts, zombies and demonic possessions. All this exaggerates the fear we have of anything beyond our physical life. In our ignorance of life and death we create a version of reality that makes us feel bad and fills us with even more fear. Yet we would never do this is we knew how important it was for us to feel good. We would not want to think and feel this way if we knew that we attract more of what we think about. If we knew that we create our reality by the thoughts we think, we might make more effort to think in a way that makes us feel good and so attract more of what feels good.

If you are able to think and believe that life is supposed to be good for you, then you will no doubt find evidence every day of how things are good for you. If you can see the hand of infinite intelligence in the wonder of life then you will find it easier to believe that life can be good for you. If you can recognise and appreciate the infinite beauty and abundance of the physical world you may find it easier to believe in even more beauty and wonder that awaits us after we die. If you can live with these positive empowering beliefs then it is possible to attract more and more happiness into your life and even to live happily ever after.

Chapter 10

Living Happily Ever After

All good stories have a happy ending but do we really believe in happily ever after? Life seems to offer little or no evidence of people living happily ever after; yet we still yearn for happiness and hold dreams of a wonderful life, where everything works out and we live happily for the rest of our lives.

The good news is that the insights and understanding presented in this book illuminate clearly how your life can be filled with happiness and good feeling. It has been shown to you that happiness is not something you have to work hard to achieve or something to search for in far away lands: happiness is at the core of your being and the very reason for life on earth.

From the outset, I have attempted to show you that life is supposed to be good for you and that the purpose of your life is to discover and experience all the joy, happiness and good feelings that you can. I have explained that there is nothing you want more than to feel good and that you have the power to create life the way you want it. So if you could have life the way you want it, how would it be? Would you want to live in a fulfilling way, filled with happiness, fun, friendship and love? Would you want to feel good about yourself? Would you want to become successful and rich? Would you want the freedom to live as you want to and to be your own boss?

If you could live a most wonderful life, where each day had something wonderful for you to experience and you felt so good most of the time would you want it to end? No, no matter how good life gets, you would just want it to carry on and get even better. And this is how it is supposed to be thanks to the law of attraction. The better your life gets, the easier it is to attract more that feels good into your life. Although, without understanding the purpose of your life, the law of attraction and how you create your life by the power of your thoughts and emotions, you may have lived your life in uncertainty and held beliefs that life is difficult, dangerous and gets worse as you get older.

The understanding in this book turns a lot

of the old ideas and concepts on their heads. Life is not about how hard you can work or how lucky you are. Life is supposed to be good for you and then by law of attraction get better and better.

As you come to understand the insights contained here you will become clearer about your purpose of life and you will begin to allow more and more good feelings and experiences into your life. You will become clearer and clearer about what you really want in life. Only when you do this can you become truly successful; for what is success other than achieving and getting what you really want. And of course, in our beautifully material world we want material wealth. We want to be rich so that we can be, do or have whatever we want. We want freedom and we want the money to express ourselves and to create and buy whatever we want. This profound feeling we have for a good and successful life is the same today as it was one hundred years ago when Wallace D. Wattles wrote in *The Science of Getting Rich*:

> *"man's right to life means his right to be free and unrestricted in his use of all things which may be necessary to his fullest mental, spiritual and physical unfoldment; or in other words his right to be rich."*

As you feel better and your life feels better,

you will undoubtedly attract material riches into your life and you will also become rich in many other ways. As you begin to see the abundance and beauty of the world we live in you will experience the richness and joy of appreciating the magnificence of life; you will enjoy the richness of wonderful friendships; you will have a rich variety of experiences and most importantly, what you want more than anything else: you will enjoy a rich variety of wonderful feelings and as you feel better and better your sense of health and wellbeing will also increase. All of this adds up to a richness of life that money cannot buy.

All of this is yours for the taking because life is made this way: life is supposed to be good for you and thanks to the law of attraction you can attract more of what you think about into your life. So as your life gets better and better you will find it easier to attract more and more of what you want; you can live an amazing life and you can live happily ever after.

Many people are striving to become rich and successful because they believe that then they will be happy; and yes along with success and riches comes some good feelings, however, this is not the whole story. Even if you are rich and successful, you could still think in ways that make you feel insecure, stressed, afraid or unhappy. Your fears could have you worrying and working relentlessly to avoid the possibility of future failure or the loss of your fortune. Instead of enjoying your wealth and prosperity you could feel bad as you worry about the deterioration of your health as you get older. Does this sound like the path to a happy ever after?

Nothing is more important to you than you feel good and the reason you want everything is because you hope to feel better when you get what you want. For example, you might want to become successful so that you can feel good about yourself and feel that your life has been well lived. You might want to be rich so that you can feel financially free and free to do whatever you want.

Since we want to feel good more than anything else it is important to prioritise feeling good and to look for opportunities to feel good throughout the day. You can decide what you do based upon how it feels and you can decide to enjoy the process as much as possible, rather than waiting for some result or accomplishment to make you feel good.

Once you understand that your purpose and priority in life is to feel good, you can discover and enjoy happiness in many ways every day. As you live this way you are living happily every day: you are already living happily ever after.

Now of course there are still ups and downs, challenges and things you want to improve. There will be some days that may feel not so good but you now have a powerful understanding that will help you through any difficult times. You understand how life works and how your thoughts and feelings create your experience. You know that life is supposed to be good for you and that the purpose of your life is to experience more and more joy, happiness and good feelings. There is no evil force waiting for you; on the contrary, the universe is on your side. When you believe this life gets very simple: as long as you are feeling good you know that you are heading in the right direction. If things don't feel that good on a particular day, remember every day is a new beginning and a new opportunity to feel good again.

There are many things in the world that you would not want in your life. There are things that you don't want everywhere but there are also things that you do want in every situation. The only question is what are you giving your attention to? For whatever you think about, you are attracting. So let us say that you are giving your attention to something you don't like or that you don't want. First of all, you will attract similar thoughts and this will not feel good. If you think more and more of what you don't want, you will be attracting it into your experience. So all you need to do is to decide that you want to feel good and let your emotions be your guide: when you are not feeling good, you know that you are thinking about something that you don't want.

If you take more control of what you are

giving your attention to and you decide to feel good; you will gain control over your emotions and your life will get better and better. As you see your days getting better you will come to see and believe that you are the only one creating your life by the way you are thinking and feeling: there is no one else controlling your life, unless you invite them in by the way you think.

When you are thinking about something you don't want for too long, it is already in your mental experience and it is affecting how you feel. If you keep thinking in this way you are attracting it or something similar into your physical experience. If you are not feeling good, this is your emotional guidance system telling you that are thinking about something you do not want. Your emotions offer you very simple, yet invaluable guidance: when you are feeling bad, you are heading towards something that you don't want and when you are feeling good, you are heading towards more of what you want. Remember, it is a happy journey leads to a happy destination.

So at every opportunity think about what you do want and seek to find positive aspects whenever you can. This may take some practise as you have created habits of thought over the years and you have probably spent quite a lot of time criticising and thinking about the many things you don't like. It will not take years to change your habits of thought but don't expect to change everything overnight. Although, after a good nights sleep is the best time to find some thoughts that feel good. You can feel positive and optimistic with each new day because now you know that your life is heading in the right direction and is improving each day. You know that every day is a new beginning and another opportunity to feel good.

Living happily ever after is not something you hope to find someday when everything is perfect, you meet the perfect person and there is nothing left to do. There will always be something else you want, something else you want to do and something you want to improve. You will also want to improve how you feel: you will still want more happiness, more passion, more excitement or more peace. You will never get to a place where you don't want or desire anything.

Living happily ever after is a way of life that you can start today. As you live in this way, feeling good more of the time, you will be attracting more and more things, people and situations that make you happy. Life just keeps getting better and better. As you look at your life, notice over and over again when you feel happy and when you notice that life is amazing in some way. As you do this day after day, you will see more and more happiness and good feelings filling your days.

So find things to enjoy, be good to yourself

and feel good. Enjoy the journey and follow your inspiration of what feels good to you. Live one day at a time and enjoy the moment. Think in a way that feels good and always give your attention to what feels good. Start enjoying your life today and enjoy watching it get better and better, in subtle ways at first, and before long you will find your life filled with happiness, freedom and joy. As you live like this, you will come to realise that you are in fact living happily ever after.

A Message from the Author

I Hope that in reading this book you have found some new and valuable insights and ways of looking at life that feel good to you. I hope you feel empowered to take control of how you feel and to make your life more the way you want it.

The ideas presented here are profound, fundamental and life changing and yet I have tried to keep my findings clear, straightforward and to the point. As I endeavoured to clarify and condense my understanding I often found myself wanting to discuss and elaborate more - there is so much more to say! This book is therefore just the beginning.

The insights found here are not just philosophical or theoretical possibilities; it has been my intention to show how these understandings can be applied to your daily life in order to produce meaningful changes in your life.

As you apply these insights into your life, you will come to understand more about yourself and what makes you feel good; you will become more sensitive to how you feel and clearer about what you want. At the same time, many more questions will undoubtedly be stirred up within you. It is therefore my intention to continue to write, explore and explain the ideas presented here. I will do this by further books, speaking events, consultations and all digital media available to us at this time.

There will a companion website, dedicated to elaborating, expanding, sharing and enjoying all that has been presented in The Most Important Hour of Your Life: www.mihour.com (from most important hour).

I hope to see you there.

Regards

Paul

December 2014

Bibliography

Atkinson, W. W. (1908) *Thought Vibration, Or, The Law of Attraction in the Thought World.* [online] Available from https://archive.org/details/ thoughtvibratio01atkigoog

Baggott, J. (2011) *The Quantum Story: A History in 40 Moments.* [Audible Audiobook] Oxford University Press.

Borgia, A. (1993) *Life in the World Unseen.* M B A Publishing.

Braden, G. (2004) *The Gregg Braden Audio Collection: Awakening the Power of Spiritual Technology.* [Audible Audiobook] Sounds True.

Byrne, R. (2006) *The Secret.* Atria Books.

Canfield, J. and Hanson, M. V. (2001) *Chicken Soup for the Soul.* HCI.

Carlson, R. (1997) *Don't Sweat the Small Stuff ... and it's all small stuff: Simple Ways to Keep the Little Things from Taking Over Your Life.* Hyperion.

Carlson, R. (1997) *Stop Thinking, Start Living Discover Lifelong Happiness.* HarperCollinsPublishers.

Carnegie, D. (1998) *How to Win Friends and Influence People.* Gallery Books.

Chopra, D. *The Seven Spiritual Laws of Success: A Practical Guide to the Fulfilment of Your Dreams.* Amber-Allen Publ. (1994).

Chopra, D. (2006) *The Seven Spiritual Laws for Parents: Guiding Your Children to Success and Fulfilment.* [Audible Audiobook] Harmony.

Chopra, D. (1990) *Quantum Healing: Exploring the Frontiers of Mind/Body Medicine.* [Audible Audiobook] Bantam.

Chopra, D. (2002) *Grow Younger, Live Longer: Ten Steps to Reversing Age.* [Audible Audiobook] Harmony.

Chopra, D. (2003) *Golf for Enlightenment: The Seven Lessons for the Game of Life.* [Audible Audiobook] Harmony.

Chopra, D. (2003) *The Spontaneous Fulfilment of Desire: Harnessing the Infinite Power of Coincidence.* [Audible Audiobook] Harmony.

Chopra, D. (2008) *How to Know God: The Soul's Journey into the Mystery of Mysteries.* [Audible Audiobook] Random House.

Covey, S. R. (2004) *The 7 Habits of Highly Effective People: Powerful Lessons in Personal Change.* Free Press.

Coelho, P. (1993) *The Alchemist.* Harper Collins.

Dass, R. (2005) *Here We All Are.* [Audible Audiobook] Hay House.

Dass, R. (1998) *Expereiments in Truth.* [Audible Audiobook] Sounds True.

Deutsch, S. (dir.) (2006) *Conversations with God.* Samuel Goldwyn Films.

Duane, O. B. (1997) *Mysticism (The Origins of Wisdom).* Brockhampton Press.

Dweck, C. S. (2006) *Mindset: The New Psychology of Success.* Random House.

Dyer, W. and Katie, B. (2007) *Making Your Thoughts Work for You.* [Audible Audiobook] Hay House.

Edwards, G. (2000) *Pure Bliss: The Art of Living Soft Time.* Piatkus Books.

Ferriss, T. (2007) *The 4-Hour Work Week: Escape 9-5, Live Anywhere, and Join the New Rich.* Crown.

Ferriss, T. (2010) *The 4-Hour Body: an Uncommon Guide to Rapid Fat Loss, Incredible Sex, and Becoming Superhuman.* Harmony.

Fox, K. (2002) *The Big Bang Theory: What It Is, Where It Came From, and Why It Works.* [Audible Audiobook] John Wiley & Sons.

Franchezzo (A. Farnese) (1992) *A Wanderer in the Spirit Lands.* Library of Alexandria.

Freke, T. and Gandy, P (2001) *The Jesus Mysteries: Was the "Original Jesus" a Pagan God?* Harmony.

Gibran, K (1923) *The Prophet.*

Goorjian, M. A. (2007) *You Can Heal Your Life* [DVD] Hay House.

Goorjian, M. A. (2009) *The Shift.* [DVD] Hay House Films.

Gray, J. (2001) *How To Get What You Want And Want What You Have.* Vermillion.

Gray, J. (2005) *Men Are from Mars, Women Are from Venus.* HarperCollins.

Haanel, C. F. (1919) *The Master Key System.* [online] Available from https://archive.org/details/masterkeysystem1919haan

Hanh, T. N. (2000) *The Art of Mindful Living: How to Bring Love, Compassion and Inner Peace into Your Daily Life.* [Audible Audiobook] Sounds True.

Hanh, T. N. (2009) *Living Without Stress or Fear:Essential Teachings on the True Source of Happiness.* [Audible Audiobook] Sounds True.

Hay, L. (2004) *You Can Heal Your Life.* Hay House.

Hay, L. (2006) *You Can Heal Your Life Study Course.* [Audible Audiobook] Hay House.

Hay, L. (1991) *The Power is Within You.* [Audible Audiobook] Hay House.

Heriot, D. (dir.) (2006) *The Secret.* [DVD] Prime Time Productions. Dragon 8 PR (original banned edition).

Hicks, E. and Hicks, J. (2004) *Ask and It Is Given: Learning to Manifest Your Desires.* Hay House.

Hicks, E. and Hicks, J. (2006) *The Law of Attraction: The Basics of the Teachings of Abraham.* Hay House.

Hicks, E. and Hicks, J. (2008) *Money, and the Law of Attraction: Learning to Attract Wealth, Health, and Happiness.* [Audible Audiobook] Hay House.

Hicks, E. and Hicks, J. (2009) *The Vortex: Where the Law of Attraction Assembles All Cooperative Relationships.* [Audible Audiobook] Hay House.

Hicks, E. and Hicks, J. (2007) *Sara, Book 1: Sara Learns the Secret about the Law of Attraction.* [Audible Audiobook] Hay House.

Hicks, E. and Hicks, J. (2007) *Sara, Book 2: Solomon's Fine Featherless Friends.* [Audible Audiobook] Hay House.

Hill, N. (1928) *Law of Success in 16 Lessons.* Available from https://archive.org/details/Law_Of_Success_in_16_Lessons

Hill, N. (1938) *Think and Grow Rich.* Available from https://archive.org/details/ThinkAndGrowRichByNapoleonHill

Holden, R. (2009) *Be Happy!: Release the Power of Happiness in YOU.* [Audible Audiobook] Hay House.

Holden, R. (2010) *Shift Happens: How to Live an Inspired Life...Starting Right Now!* [Audible Audiobook] Hay House.

Holden, R. (2011) *Follow Your Joy: 6 Creative Principles for Living a Happier Life.* [Audible Audiobook] Hay House.

Holy Bible containing the Old and New Testaments. [Authorised King James Version]

Karbo, J. (1981) *The Lazy Man's Way to Riches.*

Katie, B. (2003) *Loving What Is: Four Questions That Can Change Your Life.* [Audible Audiobook] Harmony.

Katie, B. (2006) *I Need Your Love - Is That True? - How to Stop Seeking Love, Approval, and appreciation and Start Finding Them Instead.* [Audible Audiobook] Harmony.

Katie, B. (2007) *A Thousand Names for Joy: Living in Harmony with the Way Things Are.* [Audible Audiobook] Harmony.

Katie, B. (2008) *I Wish My Body Were.* [Audible Audiobook].

Katie, B. (2008) *When Relationships Fail.* [Audible Audiobook].

Katie, B. (2008) *Fathers and Sons, Life and Death.* [Audible Audiobook].

Katie, B. (2008) *Love Stories for Fathers and Sons.* [Audible Audiobook].

Linn, D. (2005) *Journeys Into Past Lives.* [Audio CD] Hay House.

Lipton, B. H. (2005) *The Biology of Belief: Unleashing the Power of Consciousness, Matter and Miracles. Mountain of Love.*

Lipton, B. H. (2006) *The Wisdom of Your Cells: How Your Beliefs Control Your Biology.* [Audible Audiobook] Sounds True.

McKenna, P. (1996) *Supreme Self-Confidence.* [Audio CD] Paul McKenna Productions.

McKenna, P. (1996) *Success for Life.* [Audio Cassette] Nightingale Conant.

McTaggart, L. (2003) *The Field: The Quest for the Secret Force of the Universe.* [Audible Audiobook] Quill.

Millman, D. (1999) *Divine Interventions: True Stories of Mystery and Miracles that Change Lives.* Rodale Pr

Moody, R. A. (20011) *Life After Life: The Investigation of a Phenomenon - Survival of Bodily Death.* HarperOne.

Pagels, E. (1989) *The Gnostic Gospels.* Vintage.

Peck, M. S. (1978) *The Road Less Traveled: A New Psychology of Love, Traditional Values, and Spiritual Growth.* Simon & Schuster.

Earth: The Power of the Planet (2007) [DVD] London BBC.

Redfield, J. (1997) *The Celestine Prophecy.* Warner Books.

Redfield, J. (1998) *The Tenth Insight.: Holding the Vision.* Grand Central Publishing.

Robbins, A. (1992) *Awaiken the Giant Within: How to Take Immediate Control of Your Mental, Emotional, Physical and Financial Destiny.* [Audio CD] Free Press.

Robbins, A. (1996) *Personal Power II.* [Audio CD] Nightingale Conant Corp (a).

Robbins, A. (2004) *Time of Your Life*. [Audio CD] Nightingale Conant Corp (a).

Robbins, A. (2000) *Get the Edge*. [Audio CD] Guthy-Renker.

Swedenborg, E. (2000) *Heaven and Hell*. Swedenborg Foundation Publishers

Virtue, D. (2000) *Past-Life Regression with the Angels*. [Audible Audiobook] Hay House.

Walsch, N. D. (1996) *Conversations with God: An Uncommon Dialogue Vol. 1*. [Audible Audiobook] Putnam Adult. (first published 1995).

Walsch, N. D. (2005) *Conversations with God: An Uncommon Dialogue Vol. 2*. [Audible Audiobook] Hampton Roads Publishing Company. (first published 1996).

Walsch, N. D. (2005) *Conversations with God: An Uncommon Dialogue Vol. 3*. [Audible Audiobook] Hampton Roads Publishing Company. (first published 1997).

Walsch, N. D. (2002) *Friendship with God*. [Audible Audiobook] Berkley Trade. (first published 1999).

Walsch, N. D. (2000) *Communion with God*. [Audible Audiobook] Putnam Adult.

Walsch, N. D. (2004) *The New Revelations: A Conversation with God.* [Audible Audiobook] Atria Books (first published 2002).

Walsch, N. D. (2005) *Tomorrow's God: Our Greatest Challenge.* [Audible Audiobook] Atria Books. (first published 2004).

Walsch, N. D. (2007) *Home with God: In a Life that Never Ends.* [Audible Audiobook] Atria Books. (first published 2006).

Walsch, N. D. (2008) *Happier than God: Turn Ordinary Life into an Extraordinary Experience.* [Audible Audiobook] Hampton Roads Publishing Company.

Wattles, W. D. (1910) *The Science of Getting Rich* [Audio] Available at https://archive.org/details/TheScienceOfGettingRich_561

Weil, A. and Gurgevich, S. (2005) *Heal Yourself with Medical Hypnosis.* [Audio CD] Sounds True.

Weiss, B. L. (1996) *Many Lives, Many Masters: The True Story of a Prominent Psychiatrist, His Young Patient, and the Past Life Therapy That Changed Both Their Lives.* [Audible Audiobook] Grand Central.

Weiss, B. L. (1998) *Through Times Into Healing.* [Audible Audiobook] Piatkus Books.

Williamson, M. (1996) *A Return to Love: Reflections on the Principles of "A Course in Miracles".* [Audible Audiobook] HarperOne.

Wolfe, F. A. (2005) *Dr. Quantum Presents: Meet the Real Creator - You!* [Audible Audiobook] Sounds True.

Wolfe, F. A. (2005) *Dr. Quantum Presents: A User's Guide To Your Universe.* [Audible Audiobook] Sounds True.

Wonders of the Solar System (2010) [DVD] London BBC.

Wonders of the Solar Universe (2011) [DVD] London BBC.

Yogananda, Parmahansa. (1994) *Autobiography of a Yogi.* [Audible Audiobook] Self-Realisation Fellowship Publishers. (first published 1946).

About the Author

Paul is passionate about teaching the many insights he has gained in his 25 years of study into the purpose of life, what it takes to achieve success and how to find happiness.

Paul has been a teacher of Mathematics in High School and a Graphic Designer before deciding to dedicate himself to teaching his powerful insights through his writing, speaking engagements and private consultations.

Made in the USA
Charleston, SC
07 April 2015